ISBN 978-0-266-91093-0
PIBN 10089593

This book is a reproduction of an important historical work. Forgotten Books uses state-of-the-art technology to digitally reconstruct the work, preserving the original format whilst repairing imperfections present in the aged copy. In rare cases, an imperfection in the original, such as a blemish or missing page, may be replicated in our edition. We do, however, repair the vast majority of imperfections successfully; any imperfections that remain are intentionally left to preserve the state of such historical works.

(CAPE OF GOOD HOPE.)

(COLONIAL SECRETARY'S MINISTERIAL DIVISION.)

THE

ORIGIN OF THE BANTU.

A PRELIMINARY STUDY

BY

J. F. VAN OORDT, B.A. (CAPE).

Presented to both Houses of Parliament by Command of His Excellency the Governor,
1907.

CAPE TOWN:
CAPE TIMES LIMITED, GOVERNMENT PRINTERS,
1907.

[G. 17—1907.]
£42-6-3.

B.1216

PREFACE.

In submitting this Essay on "The Origin of the Bantu," for the purpose of having it printed as a Report to both Houses of Parliament, I have the honour to make the following remarks. This work is the first tangible result of three years' close and unremitted study of the Bantu question. During two of these three years, I enjoyed, through the liberality of the Government and the Parliament of this Colony, a monetary grant, which if it did not supply all my needs, enabled me to carry on my researches and to devote nearly all my time to them. Without this liberality of Government and of Parliament my work would have been impossible, and hence I consider it not only my duty to submit this Essay to Government, but I do so also in a spirit of sincere thankfulness.

It is not for me to say anything about the value of the work contained in the following pages. I gladly leave this in the hands of others, in the consciousness that I have tried to do honest and *bona-fide* work. No doubt there is much in it which will require correction in the course of time ; much will require rounding off. But the material at my disposal was scant. Beyond the valuable library which Sir George Grey left to this Colony, I had little or nothing to consult ; indeed, to enable me to become acquainted with the discoveries of the last 30 years, I have been compelled to spend a considerable sum (over £100) in obtaining the latest works from Europe. My income scarcely justified such extravagance, but rather than court disastrous failure, I have gladly made the sacrifice.

This essay purports to be a mere *Preliminary Study* on the Origin of the Bantu. Though I flatter myself that I have found the keys which will unlock most of the safes containing the secrets of Bantu philology, and of the institutions, customs, and religious ideas of that widespread race, yet the great task remains to fit these keys, and as safe after safe is opened, to spread the treasures before the scientific world, as well as before the general public.

I am determined to continue the work once begun, and to perform at least a small portion of the immense task that still requires to be done. I am doing the work from a feeling of love towards the country of my birth, as well as from a desire to serve Science ; I am prepared to devote the rest of my life to the solution of a few of the many questions which still remain unanswered.

But in order to do so, I require assistance, and principally such assistance as will put me while thus engaged beyond the sordid wants of life, and will also enable me to procure several books which I urgently require.

For these reasons I hope that the Parliament of this Colony will enable me to prosecute my researches, and to continue a work which is merely begun, and which to finish will require the energies and the time of at least a dozen more able men than myself.

I trust that I have, at all events, proved to the Government and to Parliament that the financial support they have thus far so kindly granted me has not been wasted.

J. F. VAN OORDT.

Cape Town, 28th February, 1907.

AUTHORITIES CONSULTED AND MADE USE OF.

1. Skeat and Blagden. The Pagan races of the Malay Peninsula.
2. Hodgson. Essays relating to Indian subjects.
3. Bellew. From the Indus to the Tigris.
4. Mockler. Grammar of the. Baloochee language.
5. Pierce. Description of the Mekranee-Beloochee Dialect.
6. Seymour. Grammar of the Sindhi language.
7. Clark. Ao Naga Grammar.
8. McCabe. Outline Grammar of Angami Naga.
9. Soppit. Short account of Kachcha Naga. .
10. Witter. Outline Grammar of Lhota Naga.
11. Arden's Telugu Grammar.
12. Mudaliyar. Anglo-Tamil Primer.
13. Knight, Spauldings, and Hutchings. English-Tamil Dictionary.
14. Percival. Telugu Dictionary.
15. Foucaux. Grammaire de la langue tibétaine.
16. Das' Tibetan Dictionary.
17. Jaeschke's Tibetan Dictionary.
18. Ramsay. Western Tibet.
19. Henderson. Tibetan Manual.
20. Mainwaring. Lepcha Dictionary.
21. ,, Lepcha Grammar.
22. Roberts. Anglo-Khassi Dictionary.
23. Elmslie. Kashmiri Vocabulary.
24. Wade. Grammar of the Kashmiri language.
25. Vaughan. Grammar and Vocabulary of Pushtu.
26. Elliot. Memoirs of the Races of the North Western Provinces of India.
27. Hunter. Imperial Gazetteer of India.
28. Rivers. The Todas.
29. Dirr. Annamitische Sprachlehre.
30. Wershoven. Siamesische Sprache.
31. Hepburn. English-Japanese Dictionary.
32. Seidel. Japanesische Schrift-Sprache.
33. ,, Japanesische Umgangssprache.
34. Elliot. Finnish Grammar.
35. Wellewill. Finnische Sprachlehre.
36. Meurmann. Dictionaire Français-Finnois.
37. Donner. Vergleichendes Wörterbuch der Finnish-ugrischen Sprachen.

81. Christaller. Dictionary of Asante. —
82. Reinisch. Die Barea Sprache.
83. Mitterrutzner. Die Sprache der Bari. —
84. Crisp. Notes towards a Secoana Grammar.
85. Brown. English Secwana Dictionary. —
86. Jacottet. Practical Method to learn Sesuto.
87.   ,,   Sesuto-English Vocabulary. —
88. Whitehead. Grammar and Dictionary of Bobangi. —
89. Koelle. Grammar of the Bornu language. —
90. Nylander. Grammar and Vocabulary of Bullom.
91. Mitterrutzner. Die Dinka Sprache. —
92. Seidel. Leitfaden zur Erlernung der Dualla Sprache.
93. Goldie. English-Efik Dictionary.
94. Guiraudon. Manuel de la langue foule.
95. Reichardt. Vocabulary of the Fulde language. —
96. Tutschek. Dictionary of the Galla language. —
97. Payne. Grebo-English Dictionary. —
98. Marré. Die Sprache der Haussa.
99. Robinson and Brooks. Dictionary of the Hausa language.
100. Schoen. Grammar of the Hausa language.
101. Crowther. Vocabulary of the Ibo language. —
102. Sims. Vocabulary of Kibangi. —
103. Velten. Die Sprache der Wakami.
104. Sims. Vocabulary of Kilolo. —
105. Sims. Vocabulary of Kiteke. —
106. Bentley. Dictionary and Grammar of Congo. —
107.   ,,   Grammar and Vocabulary of Luganda. —
108. Blackledge. Luganda Vocabulary. —
109. Hollis. The Masai language and Folklore. —
110. Elliot. Dictionary of the Tebele and Shuna languages. —
111. Kroenlein. Wortschatz der Khoi-Khoin.
112. Schils. Grammaire complète de la langue des Namas.
113.   ,,   Dictionaire etymologique de la langue des Namas.
114. Reinisch. Die Nuba Sprache.
115. Henry. Grammar of the Chinyanja.
116. Scott. Dictionary of the Mang'anja language.
117. Grammar and Vocabulary of Mpongwe.
118. Junod. Grammaire ronga.
119. Smith-Delacour. Shironga vocabulary. —
120. Seidel. Handbuch der Shambala Sprache.
121. Larajasse. Somali-English Dictionary. —
122. Kirk. Somali Grammar.
123. Reinisch. Die Somali Sprache.
124. Madan. English-Swahili Dictionary. —
125. Seidel. Grammatik der Suaheli Sprache.
126. Krapf. The Kisuaheli language. —
127. Stover. Observations on the Umbundu.
128. Sanders. Umbundu Vocabulary. —

129. Koelle. Grammar of the Vei language. ⌐
130. Dictionaire volof-français.
131. Boyce. Grammar of the Kafir language.
132. McLaren. Kafir Grammar.
133. Davis. English-Kafir Dictionary. ⌐
134. Grout. The Isizulu. ⌐
135. Roberts. English-Zulu Dictionary. ⌐
136. Colenso. Zulu-English Dictionary.
137. Bryant. Zulu-English Dictionary.

Besides these, use has been made of the Vocabularies found in the works of Barth, Schweinfurth, Stanley, and Johnstone, as well as of Livingstone. The above list naturally does not comprise any works on general philology, or general works on Africa, a large number of which have been perused.

CAPE OF GOOD HOPE.

THE ORIGIN OF THE BANTU.

Presented to both Houses of Parliament by Command of His Excellency the Governor.
1907.

SECTION I.

When Dr. W. H. J. Bleek died on the 17th of August, 1875, near Cape Town, the Science of Philology lost one of its greatest and most ardent students. His loss to the scientific world was particularly lamentable for more than one reason. Cut off in the midst of a great work, at an age when most men are still capable of mental and bodily exertions, he left that great work —" The Comparative Grammar of the South African Languages "—unfinished ; and what made his death most grievously felt was the fact that he left behind him nobody who was either capable or willing to continue the work so propitiously begun. Bleek was a student in the fullest sense of the word ; he was always employed in collecting new facts and data, always busy extending the already wide range of his knowledge. He never was a *teacher ;* he never trained any student ; he left no pupil or pupils to whom he had imparted any of the knowledge he had of the particular branch of Philology upon which he was engaged. The natural result of all this was, that since Bleek's death little or nothing has been done in Bantu Philology, at least not as far as independent research is concerned.

It is true, however, that in the 32 years that have elapsed since his death, we have obtained a far greater knowledge of the Bantu languages than Bleek ever possessed. With the opening up of the great centre of Africa there rose up before our eyes tribe after tribe, speaking dialects of Bantu, of which Bleek could never have dreamt. A large number of grammars, dictionaries and vocabularies have passed through the press in that third of a century ; indeed, the accumulation of new facts and data has grown to such an extent, that the most enthusiastic student finds it impossible to master even the very elementary principles of the more than 200 Bantu-dialects at present spoken over the greater part of Africa.

As is always the case in a young science, the material, at present at the disposal of the student of the Bantu-languages, is anything but homogeneous. There is, indeed, a good deal of solid, useful material, carefully gathered by competent men ; there is not a little absolutely useless stuff thrown upon the pseudo-scientific market by men who were better acquainted with the rifle than with the science of language. Above all, there is an immense amount of indifferent work collected by amateurs who meant well, and often did very fair work, but who were unable to grasp true philological principles on account of never having had any scientific training. Hence it is often the painful and laborious task of the student to separate the good wheat from the chaff. What often makes the work of the writers practically useless is their unacquaintance with the elements of phonology. Instead of following either Lepsius' system or that of the Missions (introduced by the late Professor Max Müller), several compilers of vocabularies have followed a system of their own, and, with unpractised ears, have put the most absurd sounds upon paper. So we have, *inter alia*, a vocabulary of the Kamba-language, in which some of the words end in *r*, an absolutely impossible ending for any Bantu word. To this must be added the fact that very often the spelling varies in writers of different nationalities. Where, *e.g.*, the English authors write *umbundu*, the French write *oumboundou ;* such things must not be lost sight of when we make use of valuable contributions in French, such as Junod's splendid monographies on the Ba-Ronga tribe.

It would be useless to deny that, for a considerable part of our present knowledge of the various Bantu-languages, we are to thank the Mission Societies and their workers. Wherever these men have gone, they have rightly considered it their first duty to become acquainted with the language of the people, to whom they were to preach the Gospel. As soon as they had sufficient knowledge of the particular dialect they came in touch with, they began to translate portions of Scripture ; vocabularies then followed, afterwards shorter or larger grammars, and, in many instances we find even most valuable dictionaries, based upon a careful study of the language. Koelle, Krapf, Steere, Livingstone, Boyce, Arbousset, Grout, Colenso (not to mention many more) were the first to do good and sound work. Among the many fine works of later times from the hands of missionaries we may mention Brincker's Otyi-Herero Dictionary, as well as his grammar and dictionary of Oshikuanjama ; Scott's Mang'anja Dictionary, Bentley's Dictionary and Grammar of the Kongo language, and the recently published splendid dictionary of the Zulu language by the Rev. A. I. Bryant.

In Central Africa valuable work has been done by Sir H. H. Johnston and his able assistants, who have made us acquainted with the Masai language, which, though not belonging to the

Bantu group, has had no little influence upon several Bantu languages. The Germans are also beginning to pay attention to this Central Group of Bantu, which is of the utmost importance. Yet there is a large lacuna here, waiting to be filled up, and good grammars and dictionaries of Luganda, Ki-Hima, and the dialects of the other tribes surrounding lake Victoria Nyanza, are urgently wanted.

The vast country constituting the independent Congo State is practically unexplored from a linguistic point of view, although Sims and others have made a good beginning.

In the West, from the mouth of the Congo to the borders of Liberia, and in the great Hinterland behind it, fine work has been done by the French, not only by the Roman Catholic missionaries, but also by a number of French officers, many of whom have been specially selected for this purpose by the French Government.

In Northern Rhodesia Mr. A. C. Madan is at present doing very fine preliminary work, as is proved by his recent handbooks on the Senga and Wisa dialects. But much is required to be done yet in this neighbourhood. A good grammar of Mashona is required ; or better, a series of works upon the Mashona, such as the Rev. H. Junod has written upon the Ba-Ronga. From Elliot's Dictionary of Tebele and Shuna it is perfectly clear that the Mashonas speak a most remarkable and interesting Bantu-dialect.

From the above it is apparent that the student of Bantu has at present a large amount of material at his disposal, and is thus enabled to undertake researches and reach conclusions, which Dr. Bleek could never have dreamt of. Besides this, it should be borne in mind that, since the days of Bleek, Philology has made gigantic strides. Not only have we solved the Assyrian problem to a remarkable completeness, but we have proved, thanks to Lenormant's valuable labours, that in very ancient times, about 4500 B.C., there lived at the mouths of the Tigris and Euphrates a highly-cultivated nation, the Sumerians, who spoke a language nearly related to Finnish, that is a language belonging to the so-called Ugro-Altaic group. This is a fact which, as I hope to show in this essay, is of the utmost importance to the student of the Bantu languages, a fact which will completely revolutionise our present ideas regarding this particular province of Philology.

The Ugro-Altaic group itself has been very carefully studied during the last forty years. Whatever the faults of the Government of Russia may be, want of interest in the study of the languages of its subjects in Asia has never been one of them. It has always granted ample support to students, and a mere glance at the reports and the works of the splendid Academy of Sciences at St. Petersburg is sufficient to convince anybody of the correctness of this assertion. The best dictionaries of

Mongolian, Mandchu and Turki are in Russian. Castrén, a Finn by birth, has done more to make us acquainted with the languages related to Finnish than perhaps any other scholar. The Hungarians, whose language belongs to the same group, have taken up the question in real earnest, and Vambery and Hunfalvy have done most valuable work. The Germans and Austrians have followed their lead, and at present we have a considerable number of works in German upon the subject. A small work by Dr. J. Grunzel, of Vienna, entitled : " Entwurf einer vergleichenden Grammatik der altaischen Sprachen " (1895), is perhaps one of the most concisely and clearly written books upon a vast subject, and personally I am much beholden to it, as through it my eyes were opened, and it made me see the Bantu in a clear and unmistakeable light.

Bleek was deprived of these opportunities. Indeed, he really never devoted himself to the question of the Origin of the Bantu languages. His main work was to compare a number of Bantu dialects with each other ; he moved absolutely *within* the Bantu circle. It is true that he seems to have had even as his great friend and protector, our never-to-be-forgotten Governor, Sir George Grey, an idea that there was a strong link between the languages of Africa and those of Australia, New Zealand and Polynesia. That relation *does* exist, but not in the sense usually applied to it. Bantu and Australian are but the different radii from a common Proto-Turanian centre ; hence their relationship. The fact has, however, given rise to a good deal of misapprehension, and this was not a little strengthened by the theory of the late Dr. Sclater, who placed a now submerged continent, *Lemuria*, between Africa and Australia. The Revd. A. I. Bryant has unfortunately been led astray by this theory, and in the introduction to his Dictionary of the Zulu language has ventured to assert that the Bantu moved from Lemuria into Africa. This theory must be considered as untenable in the face of the fact that the greater eastern half of Madagascar is inhabited by a nation which speaks a pure Dravidian dialect, and which, in my humble opinion, has as its fatherland the South-East coast of India. Although on the west coast of Madagascar a Bantu dialect is spoken, it is fairly certain that the tribes which speak it were originally either immigrants from Africa or, what I think more likely, were placed there against their will by the earlier Dravidian inhabitants.*

We have to look outside of Africa for the origin of the Bantu race. In trying to solve the problem we are necessarily thrown back upon the resources of Comparative Philology and,

---

* I do not consider myself qualified to pass an opinion upon the Lemurian theory, though I believe that there exists a good deal of zoological and botanical evidence in favour of it. But if Lemuria ever did exist, I am convinced that it became submerged before the human race entered upon its Western migrations.

to a small extent, upon the somewhat dangerous principles of Comparative Religion. All other resources are closed to us. The Bantu knew no other art than the making of pottery and the plaiting of mats ; several of the tribes, but not all, were acquainted with the art of melting iron ore and hammering the hot iron into weapons or implements. It may be that some of the tribes which arrived in Africa, at a later period, were acquainted with the art of weaving a rough cloth, but the evidence upon this point is not quite convincing. The Bantu have left no buildings behind them, for the huts they lived in were but frail fabrics. The antiquary will thus find little scope for his science in Africa, south of Egypt and Libya. Still less does the historian. Everything before 1500 A.D. is practically an absolute blank as far as the history of the Bantu is concerned, and the few data we have in Arabic writers about the Zanj do not throw much light upon their history. It may be, as Dr. G. M. Theal surmises, that in ancient Arabic unpublished writings, we may find something more definite about the Bantu along or near the East Coast of Africa, between Cape Guardafui and Cape Delgado. But if we do, it should be remembered that the ancient Arabic authors were not a little given to exaggeration, and were not altogether unacquainted with the " art of prevarication,' and that hence any information given by them has to be received with the greatest caution.

Philology must, therefore, be our guide, and in a case like the present it is perhaps our surest guide under the circumstances. There have been conditions under which a race has lost its original language, and has adopted the language of another race as its own. So the French, originally a Teutonic race, have adopted a Romance language ; in South Africa, the Berg-Damaras, a pure Bantu race, speak Hottentot, the language of their conquerors. On the West Coast of Central Africa, there are tribes which were probably originally pure Bantu, but which now speak a Negro dialect, and the converse case has been found too. In Fulde and in Haussa we have two languages made up of all kinds of elements—Bantu, Hamitic, Negro, Berber and Arabian. Yet there can be no doubt but that originally both the Fulde and the Haussa tribes are of true Bantu origin, though in ancient times they may have borne another name, and though a large percentage of the blood now flowing through their veins is of non-Bantu origin.

But, in general, putting extraordinary circumstances aside, a race maintains its language as one of its racial characteristics, and even political union does not always interfere with this general rule, as, for instance, is shown in Switzerland. On the other hand, it must be clearly remembered that in a race which has been subject to migrations, the language is apt to undergo various changes. Such changes are partly due to climatic influences, partly to change of customs, partly to the fact that, even if the race keeps its blood pure, the language will absorb words from other languages, so-called *loan-words*.

In Africa the Bantu became not the slaves of the indigenous races, but their conquerors, and that evidently from an early date.* But, notwithstanding that fact, the Bantu languages did absorb some part of the vocabulary of the languages of other races. In West Bantu we can clearly trace the influence of the true Negro languages ; in Central Bantu that of the Nilotic and Masai languages ; in some southern Bantu dialects we meet the clicks of the Hottentot, who though not indigenous to Africa, evidently reached that continent long before the Bantu did. In East Bantu, along the coast, there is a strong Semitic element, principally due to Arabian influence ; in Mashona there is another Semitic element, which is, however, of far older origin, and must, without the slightest doubt, be referred to Assyrian.

Yet, broadly speaking, the Bantu languages have remained remarkably pure under the circumstances, and in more than 70 per cent. of the words, we have no trouble in tracing them to their original roots.

It is quite different with Bantu Phonology. Here climatic influences and certain customs have created some of the most remarkable changes. The tribes who live on highlands have a completely different pronunciation from those who live in the lowlands or along the coast. In some Bantu languages we still find the old original *uvular r* or *gh, e.g.*, in Kafir ; while in others the *gh* has been lost and the more modern *r* sound substituted, a fact which may be due to the influence of original elements, but was probably not altogether unconnected with climatic influences.

In some tribes, who (or whose ancestors) were in the habit of knocking out their front teeth, we find *labialisation* of the *sibilantic* sounds, *i.e.*, a tendency to lisp. Thus we have in Zulu *hl* for *s*, and *thl* for an original *ts* or *g*. The custom of some tribes of boring holes in their upper lip and inserting a ring (the *pelele*) must have considerably interfered with the pronunciation of certain sounds, and made it impossible for them to sound either *p, b,* or *m* in the ordinary manner. Hence we find these letters replaced by other, often very complicated, sounds.

---

* Though I believe such to have been the general fact, I should wish to state here, that it is evident to me, that at some period or other, a section of the Bantu, including *inter alia* the ancestors of the South Eastern Bantu (Zulu, Kosa, Amabomba, etc.) was subjected by the great Masai tribe, and that this fact has not been without its influence upon the language of these Bantu tribes.

This question of Bantu Phonology cannot be treated in this essay, as the subject is too vast and far-reaching. I have only referred to it in order to show its importance, and to illustrate in how far the pronunciation, and hence the spelling of Bantu in its various dialects is affected.

The questions to be answered in this essay are :

1. WHAT IS BANTU ?
2. WHENCE DID THE BANTU RACE ORIGINATE ?

It may seem very audacious on the part of the writer to try and give the answer to these two questions, which are of such immense importance not only to South Africa and to Africa generally, but also to the Science of Philology. Yet the writer's researches and studies during an unbroken period of three years have gradually convinced him of the general correctness of his answers, and for that reason he considers it his duty to place the results of his work before the scientific public as well as before general readers.

The answers to the above questions may be conveniently gathered in the following *theses :*

I. *The Bantu language belongs to that group of languages, generally known as the Ugro-Altaic.*

II. *The fact that in the Bantu language there are two distinct groups of words, one of which is far more archaic than the other, entitles us to come to the conclusion that* • *there have been TWO Bantu invasions of Africa.*

III. *The first Bantu invasion of Africa commenced from some part in or near Hindostan, and the language of these first invaders is directly connected with the Non-Aryan languages of India.*

IV. *The second Bantu invasion of Africa started from the mouths of the Tigris and Euphrates, and probably took place about the year* 680 B.C.

V. *The real original home of the Bantu race is the Peninsula of Malacca, and the Pagan races at present found in that Peninsula are ethnographically and linguistically very nearly related to the present Bantu races of Africa.* And as a *corollary* I beg to add :

VI. *The Ugro-Altaic group of languages as well as the Bantu, which forms part of that group, have arisen from a mixture of Hamitic and Turanian elements.*

It is now my duty to adduce the proofs in support of the above assertions. In doing so, I wish to remind my readers that this essay is merely a preliminary study, and that hence I must be as succinct and short as possible. The more voluminous proofs and the more elaborate arguments in support of my theory must stand over until I am enabled to put my larger work upon the subject through the press. I am only at the very threshold of my labours, so to speak, and for that reason I have limited myself in this essay to what may be called the *lexicological* part of the Bantu languages. I have not touched upon grammatical formations, partly because my researches on this matter have scarcely begun, partly because otherwise this essay would become too bulky. I have only very slightly touched upon the important question of the Bantu *prefixes*. The object of this essay is, as said before, merely to make the philological world in particular, and the reading public in general, acquainted with a discovery, which the writer believes to be of considerable interest and scientific value.

SECTION II.

Dr. Joseph Grunzel gives on pp. 4–8 of his " Entwurf einer vergleichenden Grammatik der Altaischen Sprachen " (Wilhelm Friedrich, Vienna, 1895) a review of the different languages which belong to the so-called Ugro-Altaic group, which he divides as follows :—

I. *Uralian* or *Ugrian Group*
{ (a) Samojedian.
(b) Finnish.

II. *Altaic. Group* .. ..
{ (a) Turki.
(b) Mongolian.
(c) Tungusian.
(d) Japanese.

Each of the sub-divisions of the two groups is again split up into various languages and dialects. Thus : *Lappish, Esthonian, Permian, Votish,* as well as *Finnish* itself, belong to the Finnish group, with several others ; while *Uigurish, Kirgish, Osmanli* (Turkish) and *Tataric,* belong with many others to the *Turki* division. The *Mongolian* sub-division contains, *inter alia,* the *East*—and *West*—*Mongolian,* the *Kalmuk,* and the *Buretian ; Manchu* belongs to the *Tungusian* group, while *Japanese* forms a group in itself, but has various dialects, slightly differing from each other.*

Grunzel has not included *Accadian* nor *Sumerian* in his division, but Lenormant correctly classes these with the Uralian or Ugrian Group, and in general they seem to contain elements of both Samojedian and Finnish, and to be probably an older branch. But *Accadian,* or rather *Sumerian* (for I consider the two languages to have been originally distinct from each other, and prefer using the latter name alone, for the purposes of this Essay) had an immense advantage over the other languages of the Uralian group, in the fact that it was reduced to a system of writing, as early as 4500 B.C., and

---

* *Japanese* is generally divided into *spoken* and *written* Japanese. These differ considerably from each other, due to the influence of Chinese upon the *spoken* language.

formed what is called the Cuneiform Script. This system of writing was afterwards adopted by the Semitic races which settled in the plains between the Tigris and the Euphrates. With that *Sumerian* language we are now fairly well acquainted, though there are still a number of words or so-called *ideograms* which puzzle the best Assyriologists. Still, we know quite enough of the language and even of its grammar, to enable us to use it for comparative purposes with Bantu.

The great distinctive philological phenomena in connection with the *Ugro-Altaic* languages are the following :—

A. All syllables are open and end in a vowel. Occasionally a final syllable ends with *n* or *ng*. This is known as *nunation*. In some Ugro-Altaic languages, *e.g.* in Turkish, this rule would seem not to apply, but this exception is only apparent and not real, and the *final* vowel has really been dropped.

B. There exists a tendency to drop certain consonants between the vowels, which often results in so-called contraction. For instance :

(1) *Ugrian*	Okul	=	son.
Turkish	o–ul	=	,,
Kirgish	ūi	=	,,
(2) *Mongolian*	tak (for taku)	=	mountain.
Kirgish	ta--u	=	..
Altaic	ta	=	
(3) *Mongolian*	negu	= to stray.
Kalmuck	nou	=	,,
Buretian	nu	=	,,
(4) *Uigur*	ket (for ketu)	=	to dress.
Altaic	ke–i	=	,,
Kaschgar	ki	=	,
(5) *Mongolian*	Kube-gun	=	child.
Tungusian	kuña	=	.,
Japanese	kō	=	,,

, (This latter example is a very clear instance of a *monosyllabic* word arising by pure dropping of consonants and contraction from a *polysyllabic* word.)

C. *There is a remarkable change of consonants in several instances.* For example :

$$k = ch = g = ng = n$$
$$ch = h$$
$$g = j$$
$$t = tj = d = dj$$
$$j = ts = dz$$
$$ts = dz = s = z$$
$$l = r$$
$$z = r = l$$
$$p = f = b = v = m$$

D. *To express adjectives (and, in a few cases, even substantives) use is often made of a repetition of syllables.* For example:

Kirgish	dzibdan-dzibdan	= quick.
Altaic	akkir-akkir	= slow.
Manchu	gilta-gilta	= shining.
Manchu	bura-bara	= dark.
Osmanli	javas-javas	= slow.
Mongolian	tandur-mandur	= fright.

and many more, as given by Grunzel : *l.c.*

E. *The Ugro-Altaic languages are generally agglutinative in character, but the system of agglutination often differs in the various languages.*

F. *The Ugro-Altaic languages have no real degrees for comparison of adjectives.*

G. *The cases are formed in Ugro-Altaic languages by affixes.*

H. *The Ugro-Altaic languages have a special negative conjugation of the verb, a form unknown in any other group of languages.*

These are *some* of the distinctive peculiarities of the Ugro-Altaic languages, and if we carefully examine the Bantu languages, we shall find each of these characteristics back in the latter linguistic group.

A. *In Bantu all syllables are open and end in a vowel.*

We often find that a syllable apparently ends in *m* or *n*, the *m* being in most instances the representative of an original *n*. In reality, however, the *n* or *m* belongs to the consonant following it, and represents the *nasalisation* thereof, a feature peculiar to the Bantu group, and of pure Turanian origin.

This *nasalisation* is not found in all Bantu languages in an equal degree, nor is it easy to find any particular rule for this characteristic.

Thus we have :

Kafir	*nakuba* = although	is	Herero	*nanga* = although.
Suaheli	*butu* = blunt	,,	Mang'anja	*buntu* = blunt
Kafir	*komo* = to choose	,,	Mpongwe	*pinza* = to choose*
Kafir	(isi)*peta* = bow	,,	Suaheli	(*u*)*pindi* = how†
Mpongwe	*ompozyo* = broad	,,	Zulu	*banzi* = broad
Suaheli	*chagua* = to choose	,,	Mang'anja	*sanka* = to choose
Kongo	*kina* = to dance	,,	Herero	*punda* = to dance.

---

*For the remarkable interchange between *k* and *p*, see later on.

†In the Suaheli *upindi* we have clearly a very old form, and the *n* in this case certainly belongs to the original root, as is clear from Tibetan *phon* = archery ; Annamese *ban* = to shoot, and Sakai and Malayan *panaħ* = bow. Dualla has the oldest form of the word in *di-punga*, really meaning " the thing that is stretched." There are several words in Bantu in which such an archaic original *n* has been retained, but in present Bantu the *n* is always considered, through false analogy, as a true *nasalisation*.

A remarkable instance of nasalisation is found in Herero *oka-kambe*=a horse, which in Mang'anja is *kavalo* and in Mpongwe *kavala*, and is derived from the Portuguese *cavallo*= horse.

B. *There exists in Bantu languages a tendency to drop certain consonants between the vowels, which often results in so-called contraction.*

Thus :

Kahr	*kulu* =big	becomes Suaheli	*kuu* =big.
Zulu	*twala* =to carry	,, ,,	*twaa* =to carry.
Kaffer	(isi)*fuba* =chest	,, ,,	(ki)*fua* =chest.
Maug'anja	*kwera* =to climb	,, ,,	*kwea* =to climb.
Mang'anja	*fika* =to come	,, Mpongwe	*bia* =to come.
Suaheli	*pika* =to cook	,, Kongo	*via* =to cook.
Herero	*muna* =to discover	,, Mpongwe	*mia* =to discover.
Kafir	(in)*dlovu* =elephant	,, Secwana	*tlou* =elephant.
Suaheli	*killa* =every	,, Kamba	*kia* =every.
Herero	*tira* =fear	,, Mpongwe	*tia* =fear.

This list could be increased twentyfold without any trouble, but the above is sufficient to prove the existence of the principle, which is certainly of no little importance in Bantu philology.

C. The changes of the consonants in Bantu agree in the main with those of Ugro-Altaic, but the former has besides several other interchanges, which were common in the languages from which both Bantu and Ugro-Altaic have arisen, but which appear to have been lost (except in a very few instances) in the latter group.

The principal one of these interchanges is $k=p=b=f=d$, an interchange which had its origin in ancient Turanian where k constantly interchanges with p. B is the softer form of p, and in its turn interchanges with d, while f originated from an aspirated $p=ph$. These interchanges can be traced between Sumerian and Assyrian, and generally between the Turanian and Semitic languages.

In the Bantu languages we find them very regularly, as the following few examples out of many, will show.

Mpongwe	*ke* =also.	Kongo	*mpe* =also.
Zulu	(o)*koko* =ancestor.	Suaheli	*babu* =ancestor.
Zulu	(um)*bonda* =assembly.	Mpongwe	*nkanda* =assembly.
Zulu	*buta* =to assemble.	Kongo	*kutana* =to assemble
Kafir	*kwa* =at.	Mang'anja	*pa* =at.
Zulu	*kude* =away.	Herero	*po* =away.
Kafir	(u)*donga* =riverbank.	Suaheli	*fungu* =riverbank.
		Kamba	*kianda* =riverbank.
Zulu	*kulu* =great.	Mpongwe	(*m*)*polu* =great.
Zulu	*bopa* =to bind.	Mpongwe	*kora* =to bind.
		Suaheli	*funga* =to bind.
Mang'anja	*pa* =by.	Secwana	*ka* =by

Another change, which is not uncommon in the Dravidian languages, viz., that between *r* and *t* is sometimes found in Bantu. I have not been able to find many instances of this remarkable interchange in Bantu, but met with some noticeable instances in the Si-ronga, which has several old forms not found in any other Bantu languages. So :

Si-Ronga *rumela* = to send is Shuna *tumira* = to send.
,, *pseru* = our ,, Zulu *etu* = our.
,, *randa* = to love ,, Zulu *tanda* = to love.
,, *tatana* = father ,, Secwana *rara* = father.
Herero *tate* = father.
Si-ronga *mafura* = fat ,, Zulu (a) *mafuta* = fat.

There are some minor interchanges between letters in Bantu, which cannot be treated here, but to which attention will be drawn when they are met with in this essay.

In general the interchanges which take place in Ugro-Altaic find their counterparts in Bantu in exactly the same manner.

(a) $k = ch = g = ng = n$ (m).

Examples.

Kafir (in)*kumbi* = locust is Kamba *ngie* = locust.
Mang'anja *chambu* = medicine ,, Suaheli (u)*ganga* = medicine.
Herero (otyi) *huka* = morning ,, Mang'anja *mawa* = morning.
Mang'anja *kamwa* = mouth ,, Kamba *moomo* = mouth.
Kafir (in)*kaba* = navel ,, Herero (o)*ngna* = navel.

And many more examples could be adduced.

(b) $ch = h$.*

Examples.

Suaheli *chunga* = to nourish is Herero *hunga* = to nourish.
Suaheli *chuna* = to peel , Secwana *huna* = to peel.
Suaheli *changa* = sand , Herero (e)*heke* = sand.

(c) $g = j$.

Examples.

Suaheli *gonjwa* = sick, is Mpongwe *jaga* = sick.
Mang'anja *ganda* = to slay ,, ,, *jona* = to slay.
Kamba *guya* = to steal ,, ,, *jufa* = to steal.
Kamba *gunwa* = to drink ,, ,, *jonga* = to drink.

N.B.—In Mpongwe the *j* is really the same as a *y*, and simply another form of writing the same sound, just as we write in English **year** and **young**, but in German *jahr* and *jung*. In Mpongwe, however, the *j* is very often used as an initial letter, whilst in most other Bantu languages it is, in such position, either changed or hardened into *g* or nasalised into *ny*.

---

*In Suaheli *ch* is at present a sharp sibilantic sound like *ch* in English *church*. Originally, however, this *ch* represents (except in a few instances) an old *kh*, and this accounts really for the weakening of the *ch* into *h*. Such weakening from *kh* to *h* is very common in the Semitic languages, and *kh* in the other Semitic languages, for instance, is generally rendered in Assyrian by *h*. (See Sayce's Assyrian Grammar (1904), p. 62.) Suaheli has been strongly influenced by Semitic.

(d) $l = r$.

This is one of the most common changes in Bantu.

Mang'anja   *nyala*=hunger is Herero   (o)*ndyara* =hunger.
Kafir   (um) *kokeli* =leader ,,   ,,   (omù)*hongere* =leader.
Kongo   *tala* =to look ,,   ,,   *tara* =to look.

N.B.—In Herero the *r* (*i.e.*, the ordinary English *r*) is more frequent than in most of the other Bantu languages.

(e) $t=d$.   This is also quite common.

Kongo   *dia* =to eat is Kamba   *tiye* =to eat.
Herero (otyi)*tyitua* =fact ,, Kongo   *diambu* =fact.
Herero   (un)*dya* =to hope ,, Suaheli   *taka* =to hope.
     etc., etc.

(f) $p = f = b = v = m$.

There are a very large number of words in Bantu which show these interchanges, but the following examples must suffice :

Suaheli   *pafu* =lung.   Mang'anja   *pupu* =lung.
           Mpongwe   (i)*bobo* = ,,
Kahr   (u)*mongo* =marrow.   Suaheli   (u)*bongo* =marrow.
Mang'anja   *panga* =to make.   Secwana   *bopa* =to make.
           Suaheli   *fanya* =   ,,
           Kongo   *vanga* =   ,,
Suaheli   *pya* =new.   Mpongwe   *miala* =new.
Zulu   (isi)*balo* =   number.   Secwana   *palo* =number.
Secwana   *bona* =to obtain.   Herero   *muna* =to obtain.
           Suaheli   *pata* =   ,,
Herero   *po* =or.   Suaheli   (a)*ma* =or.
           Kongo   (o)*vo* = ,,

(g) $z (s) = r = l$.

Zulu   *ala* =to oppose. Suaheli   *zuia* =to oppose.
Kongo   *zonzeka* =to prepare. Herero   *rongera* =to prepare.
Kafir   (isi)*zatu* =proof.   Herero (otyi)*raise* =proof.
Zulu   *zika* =to sink.   Kongo   *luka* =to sink.

D. *In Bantu the repetition of syllables and words to express adjectives (and sometimes substantives) is a very common occurrence.* For instance :

Mpongwe	*ogaza-gaza*	=	active.
Herero	*kanda-kanda*	=	anxious.
Kafir	*kohlakele*	=	bad.
Zulu	(isi)*dika-dika*	=	a corpse.
Secwana	(le)*here-here*	=	cunning.
Herero	*ti-ti*	=	few.
Kafir	(i)*holo-holo*	=	hollow.
Mang'anja	(chi)*tunzi-tunzi*	=	an image.
Kafir	(u) *kwe-kwe*	=	the itch.
Mang'anja	*nya-nya*	=	..

Zulu	(i)*niki-niki*	= a rag.
Zulu	*ratya-ratya*	= rough.
Kafir	*tsaʃa-tsaʃa*	= ,,

E. *The general character of Bantu is agglutinative, but this varies in the different languages.*

This fact is so well known that it does not require any proof on my part.

F. The Bantu languages have no degrees of comparison for adjectives. Reference must be made to some other object, or the matter must be expressed by using a verb implying superiority. Thus in Kongo the sentence, " that one is the better of those two chairs," is expressed by saying : " The chairs, these two, that one has excelled in goodness," and to say, " he is the tallest of all," the expression, " he surpasses all in height " must be used. So in Herero : " I am greater than he," is *Ami omunene pu ye*, which is literally : " I am great next to him," while " he is tallest of all " is *eye omunene tyinene komeho ya avehe*, literally : " he is great very above all."

G. In Bantu there are practically at present no cases, except the *Genitive*, which is formed by a preposition or an *infix*. There is, however, strong evidence of the existence of an old affix *na*, by which a number of cases were formed. In Finnish, where we find at present 15 cases, this *na* is still found in the *Essive* case, but it is more than likely that Dr. M. Weske is correct in maintaining that in ancient Ugro-Altaic most of the cases were formed by affixing *na* or some other short affix beginning with *n*.*

In Kafir this *na*, in the form of *ni* (with occasional change of the preceding vowel) still forms the locative, just as it still does in some expressions in Finnish. So *esityeni* means " in the dish " from the noun *isitya* = dish, and I am inclined to think that in such adverbial expressions as *kona* (here, or there) and *kunye* = together, we also find this ending, the latter representing the so-called *Comitative case* (= with) in Finnish.

The subject is too intricate to be treated here in full, but certainly deserves the attention of Bantu scholars, as it throws a good deal of light upon Bantu philology.

H. Bantu, like most Ugro-Altaic languages, has a special negative conjugation of the verb, which may be considered one of the most remarkable characteristics of this group.

In Finnish we have the form *en syo* = I do not eat ; Turkish has a negative form of the verb by infixing *ma* between the stem and the affixes. So in Bantu we find a negative form of the verb, which is constituted either by a *prefix* or an *infix*.

---

*See the interesting study of Dr. *Michael Weske*, entitled " Untersuchungen zur vergleichenden Grammatik der Finnischen Sprachstammes " (Leipzig, 1873). Also C. *W. E. Elliot :* " A Finnish Grammar " (Clarendon Press, 1890), p. 23.

For instance :

Kafir	*ngi* =I am.	*angi*	=I am not.
Herero *okusuta* =to pay.		*okuhasuta*	=not to pay.
Suaheli *si piga* =I have beaten.		*si ku piga*	=I have not beaten.
Kongo *evanga* =they make.		*kevanga ko*	=they do not make.

Altogether there are very many points of similarity between the construction of verbs in Ugro-Altaic and that in Bantu, but these cannot be discussed here, without entering more deeply into the subject than can be done in this sketch. It may be mentioned, however, that in most of the Altaic languages, just as in Bantu, the *root* of the verb is usually found in the second person singular of the Imperative.

SECTION III.

If the above remarks show a remarkable similarity between the *morphology* of Bantu and that of the Ugro-Altaic languages, the *lexicological* or dictionary part, shows still stronger affinities. In most cases we find in the Ugro-Altaic languages the *same* roots as in Bantu, sometimes in exactly the *same* form, sometimes changed in accordance with the known rules of *phonology*.

I purpose giving here a short comparative list of some of the Ugro-Altaic languages and of some of the Bantu languages. As regards the Ugro-Altaic languages I am compelled at *LINE* present to limit myself principally to *Finnish* (and its immedi- *RIGHT* ately related dialects), *Turkish*, *Hungarian* and *Sumerian*, and *Japanese*, because, unfortunately, a really good Mongolian or Manchu Dictionary is not at my disposal. In the present instance I have limited myself to 100 words, taken *at random* from a far larger list in my possession, but the similarity of the root words are so strong, that even the merest *tyro* in philology must be convinced that the two language groups are intimately related. During the course of this essay several more examples will be given.

Ugro-Altaic.	*Bantu.*
1. Magyar sö-mo =the eye.	Zulu (ili)so =the eye.*
Ostiak sem = ,,	Mang'anja (di)so = ,,
2. Ugrian sul-do =cheap.	Kafir (si)-sulo =cheap.
Esthonian halv= ,,	Suaheli hafifu = ,,
Japanese (ya)-sui = ,,	

(*s* and *h* interchange in many dialects of Ugro-Altaic as well as of Bantu.)

---

*For convenience's sake I have placed the Bantu *prefixes* between ( ), so as to show more clearly the root-words. In Ugro-Altaic the *last* syllable or letter is generally an *affix*.

3. Esthonian sanaka = staff. | Zulu (um) saca = staff.
Jakutish sawa = ,, Secwana tsamma = ,,
  (w = m in most languages).

4. Finnish sapas = boot. Mang'anja (n)sapato = shoe.
Syrjenian sapoy = ,, Kongo (n)sampatu = boot.

5. Finnish sapo = dress. Secwana seaparo = dress.
(Compare Babylonian *subatu* = garment, which is evidently derived from a Sumerian root.)

6. Finnish häppo = quick. Herero haka-hana = quick.
Magyar säb = ,, Mang'anja sadiza = to hurry
                                                        (b = d)

7. Lappish oive = brain. Herero (omu)-uvi = brain.
Finnish aivu = ,,
Mordwinian ui = ,,

8. Lappish naggi = to fasten. Mang'anja (ze)nga to bind.
Mag. nugas = to fetter. | Suaheli na = to bind.
Sumerian nigin Kongo (ka)nga = to bind.
    = to surround. ;

9. Finnish nälkä = hunger. Mang'anja njala = hunger.
Esthonian nalga = ,, Herero (o)ndyara = ,,
Livonian nälga = ,, | Mpongwe njana = ,,

10. Finnish keikka = round. | Kafir (isi)giki = round.
,, kikkura = ring.
Japanese kyoku = crooked

11. Permian gögär = round. Mang'anja gango = ring.
Sirjenian gögär = ring. | Herero (o)goho = ring.

12. Finnish köna = stiff. : Zulu (lu)kuni = stiff.
,, kena = ,, | Mpongwe keta = ,,

13. Finnish jauho = meal. , Kafir (um)gobo = meal.
Livonian jouv = ,, | (g = j and b = v.)
Sumerian ku = ,, Luganda (en)gano = meal.

14. Finnish tüd = to make. ' Herero tyita = to make.
Esthonian tö = to work. Secwana diha = ,,
Mordwinian Ronga (yen)tya = ,,
    tyan = to make. | Suaheli tenda = ,,
Japanese tateru = to make |

15. Finnish tata = father. | Mang'anja tata = father
Magyar tata = ,, : Herero tate = ,,
Japanese tete-oya = ,, | Kongo tata =
                              | Rongo tata-na = ,,

16. Mongolian aχala = leader.   Mpongwe   oga = a king.
     Sumerian   aga = leader.   Luganda agalala = to sit in
                master, lord.   [state.
                                   Secwana (mog)ogi = chief,
                                            [leader.

(The root of this word is probably the Mongolian aχa = elder brother, which is found back in Suaheli (nd)ugu = elder brother, and in Secwana (nn)ake = elder brother. This very interesting word will be referred to again in a later part of this essay.)

17. Japanese   suke = to help.   Zulu   sekela = to help.
                             Isubu kalana =   ,,

(*Isubu* has clearly lost the verbal prefix.)

18. Mongolian buru-k = dark.   Mang'anja dera = dark (b = d)
     Tungusian buru = to darken   Mpongwe (m)pira = dark.
                                   Kongo   bubu = darkness.

19. Altaic   su = to love.   Herero   suvera = to love.
     Turkish sev-mek = to love.   Kongo   zola =   ,,
     Japanese   suki = to love.   Zulu   (i)su = care, attention.
     Sumerian   su = heart.

(The Herero *huura* = to love, is really from the same root, but with the interchangeable *h* form, which is found in Finnish *hywäna* = to love (= Herero *suvera*) and in Finnish *huoli* = care.)

20. Mongolian   tsirai = face.   Suaheli   sura = face.
     Buretian   sarai = face.   Aduma   (bu)shu =   ,,
     Japanese   tsura = face.
     Sumerian   suχ = face.

21. Mongolian   dobo = hill.   Zulu   (in)taba = mountain
     Turkish   dagh =   ,,   Secwana   thaba =   ,,
     Catagaish tag = mountain.   Ronga nnthunga = hill.
     Japanese   tak-ai = high.

22. Turkish   dagh = again.   Kongo   diaka = again.
     Kalmuck daki =   ,,   Luganda   daki = presently.
     Mongolian daki = to repeat   Zulu   duku-duku = to happen
                                     [shortly after each other.

23. Mongolian tusa = to help.   Secwana   thusa = to help.
     Japanese tasuke =   ,,   Kongo   (sa)disa = to help.
                              Luganda tusa = to cause to
                                        [arrive.

24. Mongol   gar = hand.   Zulu   ingalo = the arm.
     Manchu   gala =   ,,   Suaheli (m)kono = the hand.
     Turkish   kol = arm.   Kongo koko = the arm, hand.
     Finnish   koura = hand.   Oshindonga (oschi)kaχa =
                                             [hand.

25. Mongol. kundu = to adore. | Kongo   kunda = to adore.
Tungusian kundu = | Oshindonga kunda = to salute.
            adoration. | Herero   kumba = to pray.
Finnish kunnioittau
      [= to adore.

26. Mongol   kitu = to cut. | Suaheli kata = to cut.
Sumerian   χas = to cut. | Kongo kuto = sheath of a knife
Japanese kata-na = knife. | Zulu kwata = to cut all round.
Tungusian   koto = knife. | Luganda (a)kambe = a knife.
Buretian kitogo = knife. | Kikuye   kutinnia = to cut.
Finnish (lei)kạta = to cut. | Bobangi   kete = to cut.

27. Sumerian   χur = to bind. | Mpongwe   kora = to bind.
Lappish kar-et = to bind. | Secwana   golega =   ,,
Sirjenian kör-to = to bind. | (k = g ; r = l).
Buretian kulenam = | Aduma   (e)kota =   ,,
      [to bind.

28. Sumerian   χir = to cry. | Kamba   gure = to cry.
Finnish kir-jun = ,, | Zulu   kala = to scream
  | Herero   kua =   ,,
  | Oshindonga kuga =   ,,

29. Sumerian   kul = seed. | Kongo   (n)gulu = to sow.
Livonian   kull = to sow. | Herero   kuna = to sow.
  | Bobangi   (mia)kēla = to sow.

30. Sumerian kumk = finger- | Suaheli (u)kucha = fingernail.
            [nail. | Kamba   (n)gwa =   ,,
Ostiak   kunic = ,, | Haussa   kumba =   ,,
Finnish   kynsi = ,,

31. Sumerian aka = to make, | Zulu   aka = to make, build.
            [build. | Secwana aga =   ,,   ,,
Japanese ku = labour. | Suaheli aka =   ,,   ,,
  | Kamba (ku)aka =   ,,
  | Luganda   kola = to work.
  | Isubu   bola = to. make.

(The Isubu word is a very clear instance of the interchange between *k* and *b* in Bantu.)

32. Sumerian ka-ga = to name, | Kafir   (i)gama = to name.
            to call. | Secwana kua = to call.
Finnish kir-kua = to call. | Mpongwe kamba = to speak.
  | Kongo   kamba = to speak.

(The real root of these expressions is *ka* = mouth.)

33. Sumerian   ka = door   Zulu   (isi)caba = door.
    Japanese (old) kado = ,, * Kafir   (u)cango =   ,,
    Turkish   ka-pi = ,; Maug'anja   komo =   ,,
    Maqɣar   ka-puz •

34. Sumerian   kin-dea = a   Herero   (omu)kinduia = a
    messenger.   messenger.

35. Sumerian χan(hi) = a fish.   Herero   (e)hundyu = a fish.

36. Sumerian   gal = great.   Zulu   kulu = great.
                         Kafir   kulu =   ,,
                         Manganja   kulu =   ,, •
                         Secwana   golo =   ,,
                         Mpongwe (m)polo =   ,,
                                       (p = k)

37. Sumerian gim = to produce | Zulu   ki-pa = to produce.
                               Kongo   yima =   ,, (g = y).

38. Sumerian   lu = sheep.   Kamba (i)londa = sheep.
                               Zulu (uma)lusi = shepherd.
                               Bongo   romba = sheep (r = l).

39. Sumerian zun = abundant. | Kafir   zonke = abundant.

40. Sumerian kuma = to be   Zulu   pumula = to rest.
                 [quiet.   Maug'anja puma = to rest (p =
                                            [k).

41. Sumerian χi = fish.   Herero   (o)hi = fish.
                               Kamba   (i)kuya = ,,
                               Oshindonga   (o)χi = ,,
                               Wisa   •   (in) swi = ,, (ch
                                                  [= sw)
                               Oshikuanjama (o) shi = fish(ch
                                                  [= sh)

42. Sumerian sit = to protect. | Zulu   sit-elesa = to protect.

43. Sumerian an-kal = to look | Mang'anja an'gana = to look.

44. Sumerian subbu = to flee. | Kafir (uku) saba = to flee.

45. Sumerian tag = to ask.   Suaheli taka = to ask (k = g).

46. Sumerian tila = to live.   Herero   tura = to live.

47. Sumerian paga = hunger. | Zulu   (i) pangu = hunger.

---

*The word *kado* by itself is not used in Japanese, but it appears in the
expression *kado-guchi* = a door-way. The root of this word is evidently
identical with *ka* = mouth, opening.

48. Sumerian gal = to be.　　　Mang'anja kala = to be (k = g).
　　　　　　　　　　　　　　　Kongo　　kala = to be.

49. Sumerian kim = as.　　　　Suaheli　kama = as.

50. Sumerian kuku = to dress.　Zulu　g(qoka) = to dress.

51. Sumerian mul = abyss.　　　Secwana　moleto = abyss.

52. Sumerian mud-da = blood.　Secwana　madi = blood.

53. Sumerian be = blood.　　　Herero　(om)bundu = blood.
　.　　　　　　　　　　　　　Zulu　(ubu)bende = blood.

54. Sumerian kal-an = strong.　Mpongwe　(n)gulu = strength.
　　,,　　kal-ga = strength.　Kongo　　(n)gola =　　,,
　　　　　　　　　　　　　　Mang'anja　kal-am = strong.

55. Sumerian ba = to give, to　Zulu and Kafir pa = to give.
　　　　　　　　　　[bestow.　Secwana　(a)ba =　,,　,,
　　　　　　　　　　　　　　Herero & Mpongwe
　　　　　　　　　　　　　　　　　　　pa =　,,　,,
　　　　　　　　　　　　　　Suaheli　　po =　,,　,,
　　　　　　　　　　　　　　Luganda　wa =　,, (b = w).

56. Sumerian dur = to dwell.　Herero　tura = to dwell.

57. Sumerian kigar = dwelling.　Kaffir　(i)kaya = dwelling (g =
　　　　　　　　　　　　　　　　　　　　　　　　[y).

58. Sumerian uχ = flea.　　　Mang'anja ukuku = flea.

59. Sumerian ma = to call.　・Zulu　memesa = to call.
　　　　　　　　　　　　　　　(in form really a *causative*).

60. Sumerian　　　sa = to call.　Mang'anja (e)sa = to call.
　　Finnish　sa-noa =　,,　　Herero (i)sana =　　,,
　　　　　　　　　　　　　　Suaheli　(i)ta =　　,, (s = t).

61. Sumerian　pa = nose.　　Mang'anja (m)pumo = nose.
　　Sumerian　ka =　,,　　　Suaheli　　kua =　,,
　　　　　　　　　　　　　　Secwana　(n)ko =　　　,,

(Here we have a clear interchange of *p* and *k* not only in Bantu but also in Sumerian, which is of great importance.)

62. Sumerian (Gi)zug = reed.　Mang'anja (d)zogo = reed.

63. Sumerian χabir = locust.　Zulu　(in)kambi = locust.

64. Sumerian gu = to destroy.　Zulu　(i)ngozi = danger.
　　　　　　　　　　　　　　Herero (o)kuta =　,,　death.

65. Sumerian a-kal = current.	Zulu (isi)kukulu = strong cur-[rent.*
66. Sumerian bar = brother.	Manganja (m)bale = brother.
67. Sumerian bar = side. (the same word as 66.)	Mauganja (m)bali = side.
68. Sumerian sa-gal = food.	Secwana se-ya = food (g = y).
69. Sumerian mul = on.	Secwana mo = on.
70. Sumerian im = self.	Herero im = self.
71. Finnish ja = to cease.	Suaheli (i)sha = to cease. Kafir-Zulu yeka = ,,

(N.B.—In the first case the *j*, originally a sibilant, was changed into its corresponding sibilant *sh ;* in the second case, as very often happened, it lost its sibilant sound and became *y*.);

72. Finnish laka = to cease.	Mang'anja leka = to cease.
73. Finnish tuoli = a chair.	Kafir isi(tula) = chair. Secw. se(tulo) = chair.†
74. Finnish kaula = chest.	Herero (oru) kora = chest. Mpongwe (e) gara = ,,
75. Finnish powi = chest.	Zulu-Kafir fuba = chest (f = p ; b = w).
76. Finnish walikoita = to choose.	Herero vareka = to choose (v = w ; r = l).
77. Finnish kuweta = to climb	Zulu-Kafir kwela = to climb. Suaheli kwea = ,,
78. Finnish kappa = mantle.	Zulu-Kafir (in)gubo = mantle. Secwana kobo = ,,

*In the Sumerian word the *a* belongs to the root, for *a* = water and *kal* = strong. In Zulu the first *k* of *kukulu* is probably affixed, or the prefix was rather *ku*, so that we would have *ku-akulu = kukulu.* Later on the fact that the word really had a prefix already was lost sight of, and a later prefix *isi* added.

†It is quite possible that the Kafir and Secwana words are mere adaptations of the Dutch word *stoel* = chair, and that on the other hand the Finnish word is also a Teutonic loan-word, as many other Finnish words are. The Finnish may, however, be directly derived from the Turanian root *tho* = to raise, from which probably our *throne* (with the usual inserted r) is derived. The Mpongwe (*sa*)*tanga* and the Ronga (*shi*)*tama*, which may be related to the Finnish, are certainly not derived from the Dutch. I believe that the chances are that the Kafir and Secwana words *are* of Dutch origin.

79. Finnish watteus = clothes. | Kongo (mo)watu = clothes.
| Kafir (izi)vatu = ,,
80. Finnish tulla = to come. | Secwana tla = to come.

81. Finnish sääliä = to com- | Zulu sola = to complain.
[plain. | Zulu (i)silola = a complaint.

82. Finnish sakkoon = to con- | Secwana sekisa = to condemn.
[demu. | Suaheli hukumu = ,, *

83. Finnish wamma = damage. | Kafir (uk)wona = damage.
| Suaheli vunja = ,,

84. Finnish häta = danger. | Herero o-kuta = danger.
| Suaheli hatari = ,,
(See No. 64, where the probably older Sumerian form is given.)

85. Sumerian me-lam = day. | Zulu (u)muhla = day.
Finnish wa-lo = ,, | Kongo lumbu = ,,

86. Finnish sämpää = button. | Kongo sumbo = button.

87. Finnish pukea = to bury. | Herero paka = to bury.

88. Finnish mytty = bundle. | Secwana ṅata = bundle.
(ṅ = ny.)

89. Finnish (ky)psya = to burn | Mang'anja psya = to burn.

90. Finnish sywä = deep. | Zulu suve = deep.

91. Finnish synkka = deep. | Kongo (a)xinga = deep.

92. Finnish kokko = peak. | Zulu (isi)gonga = peak.
(N.B.—In these two last examples the *kk* in Finnish changes into Bantu *ng*, which is in perfect harmony with the phonology of the latter group.)

93. Finnish kunta = family. | Herero (otyi)kutu = family.

94. Esthonian kaza = wife. | Herero (omu)kazendu wife.
| Kafir (in)kazana = ,,
| Kafir kazi = female.

(The etymology of Herero *omukazendu* is as follows : *omu* = article + prefix for human beings ; kaza = woman or female ; *ndu* = person.)

---

*Although the Suaheli *hukumu* would agree letter for letter with Finnish *sakkoon*, it may be that the former word is a direct adaptation of the Arabic *hakam*, from which language many words have been taken over in Suaheli.

95. Finnish kisa = to dance.   Suaheli   chesa = to dance.

96. Ostiak sana = fine.   Secwana se-sane = fine.

97. Finnish säülü = care.   Kafir i-xala = care.

98. Sirjenian si = sound.   Zulu   (um)sinda = sound.

99. Livonian ibus = hair.   Kafir (u)baya = hair.
        abbon = beard.

100. Sirjenian   si = a hair.   Mang'anja tsi-tsi = hair (plural)
     Permian   si = ,,

Although there may be in the above list a few words, the connection of which might appear doubtful, the vast majority certainly tend to show how intimate the relations are between the Ugro-Altaic languages and the Bantu languages.

It will be seen that in Sumerian, as in a few other languages of the Ugro-Altaic group, there seems to be a tendency to end the words and syllables in consonants instead of keeping them open. But this tendency is possibly only *apparent*, for we are only able to read Sumerian by the light of Cuneiform script, and it is, in my opinion, still a question whether, in pronouncing the words, the Sumerian did not add a vowel after the last consonant.

It will also be noticed that a large number of Bantu words are directly traceable to Sumerian, with but *very slight changes*, and hence the question arises, whether we are on that account entitled to consider the Bantu, or, at all events, a considerable portion of them, as direct descendants from a Sumerian stock. This question will be treated in this essay at a later stage, but here we have first to consider another and more immediate question.

The fact that in the above list there is such a marked similarity between the Bantu *roots* and the Ugro-Altaic *roots*, must not lead us to the conclusion that *Bantu is derived from Ugro-Altaic*. This would be a serious ethnological mistake, for the differences between the two races, from a physical and ethnological point of view, are too wide for such an assumption. The Finns, for instance, and their nearest relations, the Sirjenians, have an undoubted strain of Aryan blood in their veins, and Aryan influence is also traceable in their language. In the Mongolian, Manchu, Jakutian, Tungusian and Japanese members of the Ugro-Altaic ethnological group there is a strong strain of what is generally called the *Mongolian or Tataric element*, an element which is at present not easily defined, but which would seem to be connected with the influence of an ancient Malayan race.

The Bantu have no strain of Aryan blood, as far as we can find out, nor do they show the marked characteristics of the Mongolian group, such as for instance the greater .or less obliquity of the eyes, though this was, to some extent possessed by the races which in the very oldest times inhabited the country near the mouths of the Tigris and Euphrates.

The proper view to take, therefore, of the question in hand is to consider that both the Ugro-Altaic race and the Bantu race sprang from *one common stock*, centuries and centuries ago. When they parted from that common stock cannot be definitely fixed, but considering the fact that the Sumerians are known to have inhabited the country near the mouths of the Tigris and Euphrates as early as 5000 B.C., we must come to the conclusion that Bantu and Ugro-Altaic had then already entered each upon their own path of development.

In a matter like this historical ground fails us altogether. It is true that we may be able to trace certain myths, but after all the only sound footing we have is in the department of Philology, and we are absolutely limited in our researches to that department, though able, here and there, to call the somewhat uncertain science of Anthropology to our aid.

In doing so, we are at present compelled to take a jump, and to skip, for the nonce, certain intermediate stages which will be treated of afterwards.   I must therefore ask my readers to accompany me to the Malacca Peninsula, where I believe we will find the origin of the Bantu.

SECTION IV.

In August, 1906, there appeared in England a book which, in a remarkable degree, combined that practical view of matters, so characteristic of the Anglo-Saxon, with the sound scientific scholarship one is accustomed to meet with in German and French works and which (alas!) has been so often found wanting in even the best English works. The title of this work is " The Pagan Races of the Malay Peninsula," and the authors are Messrs. *W. W. Skeat* and *C. O. Blagden.** The former is already well known to the general English public as a man intimately acquainted with the Malay language and Malay magic. Mr. C. O. Blagden has been known to the scientific world as a valuable contributor to the Journals of the Royal Asiatic Society, especially to the " Strait Settlements " branch thereof, and his co-operation with Mr. Skeat in this valuable work considerably enhances the value thereof.

*The publishers are Messrs. McMillan and Co., London, and the work is a credit to this already renowned firm. The works (two volumes, at 21s. each) are splendidly illustrated, and printed very nearly without a single mistake.

It is impossible for me to give even a short *resumé* of this work in these pages, and I must refer my readers to the work itself. I can only state here the bare facts.

In general the Pagan inhabitants of the Malacca Peninsula can be grouped under three headings, viz. :—

A. The Semang.
B. The Sakai.
C. The Jakun.

Though, as the authors have very clearly shown, there are large portions of the Malacca Peninsula in which the three races have more or less blended, the characteristics of each race can yet be easily traced in several tribes, which have kept themselves fairly pure. These characteristics may shortly be defined as follows.*

A. *Semang Type.*—Height of men about 1,491 mm.; of women 1,408 mm.; skull-index brachyo-cephalic (or bullet-headed) to mesaticephalic ; skin of a dark copper or rather chocolate-brown colour, passing into a " shiny black "; hair (which is generally shaved off) woolly, like that of the Negro and the Papuan ; forehead low and rounded ; nose remarkably broad and flat or " spreading "; cheeks full, but with the cheek-bones not very prominent ; eyes round, wide open, and straight (*i.e.*, not oblique like those of the Mongolian races) ; chin feebly developed (*i.e.*, rounded off, and frequently almost unmarked) ; mouth variable, but rather large as a rule, the lips, which are also variable, being generally well formed, but sometimes turned outside or " everted " ; beard, none to speak of, as a rule, but when found, thin and straggling, or, occasionally woolly like the hair itself.†

B. *Sakai Type.*—In height the Sakai are, I think, without doubt, a slightly taller race than the Semang or Negritos. The shape of their head, on the other hand, is in marked contrast to that of the Negritos, as they belong in type to the dolichocephalic, or long-headed races. Their skin-colour varies more remarkably than that of any of these tribes, being in some extremely dark-brown, in others a remarkably light yellowish-brown, much lighter than that of the Malays. Their hair, too, is long, black, and wavy in character, sometimes with a slight reddish tinge in reflected light. Their forehead is flat, and projects remarkably over the root of the nose, which latter is, as a rule, somewhat fine and small, and often slightly tilted at the tip. The cheek-bones are very

---

*For particulars and for the fine portraits of the various races I must again refer the reader to the work itself.

†This description, as well as those of the Sakai and Jakun, have been taken *verbatim* from Skeat and Blagden's above work, vol. I., pp. 34-36. In the appendix to the work, pp. 573-602, the reader will find very valuable further anthropological data, which I could not take up in this sketch, but which contain much information from the hands of Professor Virchow.

broad, especially when considered in relation to the rest of the features. Their eyes are a very dark brown, small, horizontal, and often half closed, as different as can be from those of the Semang. Their chin is long and somewhat sharp and pointed. Their mouth is of small size, with lower lip full, loose, and often conspicuously projecting. Their beard is, as a rule almost non-existent, but a few individuals occur who are fairly well covered with hair.

C. *Jakun Type.*—In height the Jakun appear to be, if anything, a little taller than the Sakai (in which case they would be the tallest of the three aboriginal races). Their head is brachycephalic or "bullet-shaped.". Their skin is generally of a dark coppery colour, not unlike that of the Malays, but with a tendency to darker shades, which are, doubtless, due partly to exposure and partly to their manner of living. Their hair is long and straight, or "smooth," and of a dark bluish-black tint, such as is invariably found in the hair of Mongolian races. Their forehead is usually well developed. Their nose is, as a rule, thick, flattish, and short, with wide open nostrils, though it must be noted here that a more developed type occurs. Their cheekbones are very high and well marked, like those of the Mongolian type. The face, as a rule, is inclined to be flattish. Their eyes are dark brown, of moderate size, and rarely with some slight tendency to obliquity. They have, as a rule, a strong chin and somewhat square jaws. Their mouth, as a rule, is large and broad, though frequently moderate and with well-formed lips. Their beard is of the scantiest.

Thus far the authors of the "Pagan Races of the Malay Peninsula."

In the appendix to Vol. I. the following data are given :

Semang. Cephalic index : 78.9 ; 81.1 ; 74.4 ; 80.6 ; 81.6 ; 85.

Sakai. Cephalic index : 77.4 ; 76.1 ; 73.8.

Jakun. Cephalic index : 76.7 ; 83.3.

      Capacity :

Semang. 1245 c.c. ; 1425 c.c.

Sakai. 1370 c.c.

Jakun. 1032 c.c. ; 1190 c.c. ; 1230 c.c.

As I do not lay claim to any but the most superficial knowledge of the science of Anthropology, I shall not discuss these figures, but I beg to express an opinion that it would be well if some South African scientist, who is acquainted with Anthropology and skull measurements, would go to the trouble of comparing with each other these figures with :

    (*a*) The known figures of the non-Aryan races of India.

    (*b*) The known figures of the Hamitic races, *i.e.*, Galla, Somali and Abyssinians.

(c) The known figures of the Hottentot, the Bushman, and the principal Bantu tribes.

(d) The known figures of the true African negro.

(e) The known figures of the principal Ugro-Altaic tribes and races.

I venture to think that a careful examination and comparison of the anthropological data of these races would lead to very important results.

Leaving such researches to men who are better qualified than the writer, I must now return to the discussion of my own department, that of languages. I have drawn up a very careful list of Bantu words and of words of the three languages of the Malay Peninsula, and I confess that the results were somewhat startling to me. As I wish to show how I came to these results I beg to give here a list of some words. On the left side will be found the *Malacca* words, on the right side the *Bantu* words, and here and there I have given some illustrations from other Ugro-Altaic languages. The list is by no means complete, but it is quite large enough for practical purposes, and certainly tends to show what the relations are between the races of Malacca and the Bantu races, and how far their lexicological affinities extend. ·

SECTION V.

Malacca.	*Bantu.*
1. Sakai *pela* = to abandon.	Bobangi *kila* = to abandon (p = k).
2. Semang *jā* = to abandon.	Zulu (*shi*)*ya* = to abandon.* Kafir (*uku*)yeka = ,,
3. Semang *pe* = above.	Zulu *pe*-(*zulu*) = above in the heaven. Wisa *pa* = above.
4. Sakai *puru* = abscess.	Bobangi *mpòta* = abscess (r = t).
5. Semang *tueh* = afraid.	Luganda *tya* = to be afraid. Mpongwe *tia* = afraid. Shuna *tya* = to be afraid. Haussa *tuizera* = afraid.
6. Semang *te-koh* = after- [wards.	Ronga (*an*)*thaku* = afterwards.

---

*The *shi* in Zulu is naturally no *prefix* here, but probably means " a thing," so that the word is a compound one, meaning " to abandon a thing."

7. Sakai *pula* = again.

Umbundu (*olu*)*wali* = again.
(p = b = w).
Oshikuama *vali* = again.
Aduma *bua* = again.

8. Semang *ga-ga* = strong.
(reduplication of root *ga*.)

Kongo (*a*)-*ngo-lo* strong.
Wisa (*a*)-*ko-sa* = strong.
Luganda *gu-mir* = strong.
(N.B. *mir* = *man*.)
Oshindonga (*zi*)-*gu*.
Compare Sumerian *gal* =
[strong.

9. Semang (*ya*)-*sol* = to stroke

Secwana *shola* = to stroke.
Tebele (*e*)*sula* = ,,
(Japanese *sasura* = ,, *)*

10. Sakai *posh* = storm.
pāa = ,,
pui = ,,

Zulu (*isi*)*pepo* = storm.
Kafir (*isi*)*pango* = storm.
Wisa (im)*pepo* = storm.
(Sumerian *papa* = storm.)

11. Semang *begiyu* = storm.

Luganda (*ki*)*buyaga* = storm.
(*omu*)*yaga* = storm.
(with metathesis of *y* and *g*.)

12. Sakai *helu* = storm.
hal-hül = ,,
(with reduplication.)

Mpongwe (*o*)*gula* = storm.
(Sumerian *im-hul* = storm.)

13. Sakai *dudao* = stick.

Mang'anja (*n*)*dodo* = stick.
Kamba (*n*)*deta* = stick.

14. Sakai *lu-dal* = stick.

Luganda (*o*)*luga* = stick.
Zulu (*u*)*luti* = ,,

15. Semang *balu* = stone.

Zulu (u)*mbele* = stone.
Manganja *mwala* = ,,
Dualla (i)*dali* = ,, (d = b)

16. Semang (ya) *nyan* =
[to stand.

Zulu *mana* = to stand.
(ny = m).
Kamba (u)*ngema* = to stand.
(ny = ng).

17. Sakai *jin-juk* = to stand.

Kongo *jujila* = to stand.
(with metathesis ?)

18. Sakai *pit* = to squeeze.

Secwana *pit-la* = to squeeze.
Botangi *pioto* = ,,

19. Semang *pia* = to squeeze.	Wisa *fina* = to squeeze (p = f).
20. Sakai *kenan* = to squeeze.	Zulu *ka-ma* = to squeeze. Manganja *kanikiza* = ,,
21. Sakai *baru* = a plain.	Secwana (lo)-*bala* = a plain (r = l).
22. Semang *wau* = a dog.	Herero *mbua* = a dog (w = mb). Secwana *mbwa* = a dog. (and in several other languages.)
23. Sakai *cha(cho)* = dog. *chau* = ,, Semang *chu* = ,,	Kikuya *chui* = dog. Zulu (i)*govu* = ,, (ch = g). Mang'anja *garu* = ,, (ch = g). Kamba *solu* = ,, (ch = s). (Compare Sumerian (*ur*)*chu* = dog).
24. Semang *nyang* = dog.	Zulu (i)*nja* = dog. (Compare Japanese (i)*nu* = dog).
25. Semang '*mpa* = to dream.	Zulu *pupo* = to dream.
26. Sakai *nyo* = to drink.	Herero *nua* = to drink. Secwana *nwa* = ,, Mang,anja *mwa* = ,, Luganda *nywa* = ,, (Japanese *nomu* = ,,)*
27. Sakai *ngun* = to drink. (another form of No. 26.)	Kamba *gunwa* = to drink. Aduma *egnua* = ,,
28. Jakun *jo-oi* = to drink.	Mpongwe *jongo* = to drink. (Syrjenian *juny* = to drink.)
29. Sakai *kara* = to dwell.	Herero *kara* = to dwell. Kongo *kala* = ,, Suaheli *ka-a* = ,, Shuna *gara* = ,, (g = k).
30. Semang *ya* = to dwell.	Secwana (a)*ga* = to dwell (g = y). Zulu (a)ka = to dwell.

*The old form of the Sakai is actually found back in the Dualla *nyo* = to drink.

31. Sakai *ba, be, bi, bo, bu** = father.   Zulu   *ubaba* = father.
(See *Skeat and Blagden op. cit.* II., page 598.)   Kafir   *ubawo* = ,,

31. Sakai *ba, be, bi, bo, bu** = father. (See *Skeat and Blagden op. cit.* II., page 598.)	Zulu *ubaba* = father. Kafir *ubawo* = ,,
32. Semang *ta* = father. Sakai *ta-ta* = ,,	Herero · *tate* = father. Mang'anja *tata* = ,, Dualla *tite* = my father. Kongo *ta-ta* = father. Isubu *te-ta* = ,, And many more languages, both in Bantu and in Ugro-Altaic. Secwana *rara* and Mpongwe *rere* are probably the same forms, where the *t* has been changed into *r*.† Luganda *kitanga, kitawe*, etc., probably belongs to this group, though the prefix *ki* seems inexplicable here.
33. Sakai *mahitn* = fat (adj.)	Zulu *amafuta* = fat (n).† Mang'anja *mafuta* = ,, (n). Secwana *mahura* = ,, (n). Luganda *amasavu* = ,, (n) (h = s). Ronga *mafura* = fat (n).

34. Semang *mji* = fat (adj.).
     meche =   ,,
	Kongo *amaji* = fat (adj.).
	   ,, *maji* = fat (n).

35. Semang (en)*cha* = fat(adj.) Sakai *be-cho* = fat(adj.)	Shuna *kora* = to be fat. Herero *e-kara* = fat (adj.). Bobangi *bakatala* = to be fat.
36. Sakai *gemu* = fat (adj.)	Luganda *-gevu* = fat (adj.) [Compare with 33-35. Japanese *koeta* = fat (adj.) Manchu *hetu* = ,, ,, Sumerian (nu)-*chu* = ,, (n) Jakutish *sia* (for jia) = ,, (adj.)]

---

*These rootwords, which include the whole scale of vowels, are of great importance, and tend to show that at any rate in these and related groups "vowels cannot be considered as fixed elements of the language," but that they are changeable as circumstances demand. Such would be in absolute agreement with the *Vowel-harmony* of the Ugro-Altaic languages, of which traces are found in Bantu.

†These and the examples given under No. 34 show that the fact that *amafuta* is now in Bantu considered as a *plural* noun, is simply the result of false analogy, based upon the supposed prefix *ama.*

37. Sakai   *jaras* = finger.   Mang'anja   *chala* = finger.
    Luganda   (en)*galo* = finger.

38. Semang *chand-ras* = fingernail.   Suaheli   *chanda* = finger.

39. Semang *tik* = hand.   Ronga   (li)-*tiko* = finger.
(In several old languages the words for " arm," " hand," " finger," are confused or intimately connected.)

40. Sakai   *ayam* = fowl.   Kongo   *eyembe* = fowl.
    Luganda   *enyonyi* = ,, (?)

41. Sakai   *dena* = fowl.   Herero   *ondera* = fowl.
(Compare Japanese *tori* = fowl.)

42. Sakai *puk: pok: pup: keok:* = fowl.

N.B.—The form *keok* is found in only *one* dialect, but it shows the tendency to interchange *p* and *k*.

    Zulu   *inkuku* = fowl.
    Kafir   *inkuku* = ,,
    Mang'anja   *nkuku* = ,,
    Secwana   *kok* =
    Luganda   *enkoko* = ,,
    Suaheli   *kuku* = ,,
    Wisa   *nkoko* = ,,

43. Sakai   *seng* = forest.   Zulu   (i)*singa* = forest.
    Secwana   *sekgwa* = ,,

44. Jakun   *hu-tan* = forest.   Herero   (otyi)*hua* = forest.
    Oshidonga (oshi)*chua* = ,,
    Wisa   (i)*chonde* = ,,
    Mpongwe   (i)*ga* = ,,
(Compare Finnish *kaira* = forest.)

45. Semang   *maku* = egg.   Manganja   *maika* = egg.
    Isubu   *moko* = ,,

46. Sakai   *tab* = egg.   Kamba   *itumbi* = egg.
    Ronga   *tanda* = ,,
(Compare Japanese *tamago* = egg.)

47. Sakai   *zai-s* = blood.   Luganda   (omu)*sai* = blood.

48. Semang   *yap* = blood.   Zulu   (i)*gazi* = blood.
    Kafir   (i)*gazi* = blood.

49. Sakai   *hawa* = air.   Suaheli   *hewa* = air.
(Compare Turkish *hewa* = air.)

50. Semang *mühai* = air.

Luganda	(o)*muka* = breath
Zulu	(u)*moya* = air.
Mang'anja	*mpweya* = air.
Secwana	*moea* = air.

51. Sakai   *tela* = arrow.

Kafir   (u)*tolo* = arrow.

52. Semang *halag* = lizard.

Oshindonga   *ekalala* = lizard.
                     (*k* = *h*).

53. Sakai *huwah* = to love.

Herero *suvera* = to love (*s* = *h*).
    „   *huura* =   „   „
(Comp. Japanese *horeru*
              = to love.)

54. Sakai   *hok* = to love.
(Probably another form
of 53.)

Oshindonga	*chola* = to love.
Oshikuanjama	*hola* = to love.
Luganda	(a)*gala* = to love.

55. Sakai *paā, pai* = new.

Suaheli	*pya* = new.
Wisa	*pya* = new.
Herero	*pe* = new.
Mang'anja	(tso)*pana* = new.

56. Semang *her-*(kut)
               = night.

Luganda (e)*kiro* = night (*h* = *k*)

57. Semang *tu-woi ; tu-wi*
               = night.

Herero   (ou)*tuku* = night.

58. Sakai   *lu* = pig.

Mang'anja	(ngu)*luwe* = pig.
Ronga	(ngu)*lubele* = pig.
Zulu	(ingu)*lube* = pig.*

59. Sakai   *bis* = pig.

| Luganda | (em)*bizi* = pig. |
| Herero | (um)*binda* = pig. |

60. Sakai   *kumo* = pig.

Wisa	(in)*kumba* = pig.
Mang'anja	(n)*kumba* = pig.
Kafir	(i)*hangu* = „ (?)
	(*h* = *k*).

61. Semang   *pe* = to cook.

Zulu   *peka* = to cook.

62. Semang *sema* = all.

Suaheli   *zima* = all.

63. Sakai   *kilé* = angry.

Wisa	(u)*kali* = anger.
Bobangi	*nkelele* = anger.
Kamba	*killalu* = angry.
Suaheli	(u)*kali* = anger.
Luganda	(e)*kiruuru* = anger.
	(*r* = *l*).

---

*In Sakai *gau* is also " pig," and it is quite possible that the above three Bantu words are a compound of *two* repeated words meaning the same, a linguistic phenomenon not uncommon in Eastern language. Kamba has for " pig " *ngue*, which is clearly related to *gau*.

64. Sakai	*jeboh* = arm.	Suaheli	*guba* = arm.	

65. Sakai	(a)*bu* = ashes.	Mpongwe	(o)*mbu* = ashes.	
		Luganda	*e'vu* = ,,	
			(b = v).	
		Isubu	(di)*bu* = ashes.	

66. Sakai	*charu* = bed.	Secwana	*sealo* = bed.	

67. Sakai	*bok* = to bind.	Zulu	*bopa* = to bind (k = p).	
		Secwana	*boha* = ,, (k = h).	

68. Sakai	(che)*kat* = to bind.	Aduma	*ekota* = to bind.	
		Bobangi	*koto* = ,,	

69. Sakai	*kage* = to bite.	Aduma	(e)*kaga* = to bind.	

70. Sakai	*'lemun* = tooth.	Zulu	*luma* = to bite.	
	lemuin = to bite.	Kafir	*luma* = ,,	
		Luganda	*luma* = ,,	
		Secwana	*loma* = ,,	
		Oshindonga	*lumàna* = ,,	

71. Sakai	*ku* = at.	Luganda	*ku* = at.	
		Wisa	*ku* = ,,	
		Umbundo	*ko* = ,,.	
		Secwana	*kwa* = ,, .	

72. Sakai	*ba-kul* = basket.	Bobangi	(e)*bŏkŏ* = basket.	
		Kongo	(m)*bango* = ,,	

73. Sakai	*hongmeng* = bat.	Zulu	(i)*gomongo* = bat.	

74. Sakai	*ti* = to be.	Mang'anja	*ndi* = to be	
		Herero	*ri* = ,, (t = r).	
		Wisa	*li* =	

75. Sakai	(en)*tu* = breast, chest.	Adumi	*tulu* = chest.	
		Bobangi	*ntolo* = ,,	
		Kongo	*tulu* =	
		Oshindonga	(oñ)*tulo* = ,,	

76. Sakai	*bu* = female breast.	Zulu	(i)*bele* = breast.	
		Kafir	(ama)*belc*.	
			= breast (plural)	
		Luganda	(e)*bere* = breast.	
		Bobanbi	*libele* = breast.	
		Dualla	(di)*be* = ,,	

77. Sakai	*bah* = brother.	Mang'anja (*m*)*bale* = brother. Kongo (m)*bungi* = ,,
78. Sakai *kolo* = elder brother.		Zulu (um)*kuluwe* = elder brother. Oshikuanjama (omu)*kulu* = elder brother. Aduma (mu)*kulu* = elder brother.
79. Sakai *chengru* = to call.		Suaheli *changa* = to call. Mang'anja *chemera* = ,, Herero (i)*sanga* = ,,
80. Sakai	*kap* = to catch.	Secwana *kapa* = to catch.
81. Sakai	*kat* = to catch.	Zulu (qa)*kata* = to catch. Mpongwe *kota* = ,, Wisa (i)*kata* = ,, Oshikuanjama *kuata* = ,, Luganda *kwata* = ,,
82. Sakai	*yak* = to come.	Herero *ya* = to come. Bobangi *ya* = ,, Oshindonga *ja* = ,, Luganda *ja* = ,,
83. Sakai	*bai* = to boil.	Zulu *bila* = to boil. Kafir *bila* = ,,
84. Sakai	*tohop* = to boil.	Luganda *tokota* = to boil.
85. Sakai	*san* = boy.	Shuna (mli)*sana* = bay. Herero (omu)*zandu* = ,,
86. Sakai	*hub* = breast.	Secwana (se)*huba* = breast. Zulu (isi)*fuba* = ,, Suaheli (ki)*fua* = ,, Luganda (eki)*fuba* = ,,
87. Sakai	*buta* = blind.	Zulu (*m*)*pute* = blind. Herero *potu* = ,, Bobangi *poto* = ,,
88. Sakai	*kouat* = companion.	Herero (*omu*)*kuao* = companion. Luganda (omu)*kwano* = companion. Oshindonga (o)*kuume* = companion. Shuna (m)*kwamjina* = companion.
89. Sakai	*sika* = to come.	Mang'anja *fika* = to come (f = s). Tebele *figa* = ,,

In the above list I have only taken up a certain number of words, which agree *both in form and meaning*, but if *related* meanings and somewhat *divergent* forms were taken up in it, the list could easily be brought to include 400 or 500 examples.

It has been said that *language* in itself does not prove anything, but in cases where such *complete harmony* exists as in the above list, I think the statement requires some qualification.

But it could be shown that a good deal of the customs of the Bantu races may be traced in origin to the Semang and the Sakai. The former build " beehive " structures, like our Southern Bantu ; the latter build the rectangular oblong huts found ·in Central and East Africa. Many of the marriage customs between the races agree, and the " spirit and ancestor-worship," are found in the Malacca Peninsula as well as in Africa. Even the painting or " smearing " the body with white paint or clay is used in certain religious or quasi-religious ceremonies by the Semang and Sakai, just as is done at present at the circumcision rites in several Bantu tribes.

Yet it would be a mistake to suppose that the *Semang* and *Sakai* ever came from the Malacca Peninsula to Africa. On the contrary, I am convinced that many centuries passed before the ancestors of the present Semang and Sakai, who left the Malacca Peninsula thousands of years ago, reached Africa. But this important subject requires some paragraphs of its own.

SECTION VI.

Messrs. Skeat and Blagden's book contains in Vol. II., pp. 379-472, a very valuable introduction to the study of the languages of the Malay Peninsula. They rightly class these languages under the so-called *Mon-Annam* family, a name given originally by *Logan*, but often called on the Continent the *Mon-khmer* family. Both names are not very fortunate, as they really denote an artificial mixture which, in fact, does not exist.*

That the language of Annam is probably a *purer* language than the languages of the Malacca Peninsula, I am convinced ; but I do not think that this entitles us, as both the above-mentioned authors and that great authority *Schmidt* do, to come to the conclusion that the Malacca Peninsula was invaded by a *Mon-Annam* race *from the North*. On the contrary, I am of opinion that the opposite has taken place, and that the

---

Annam or *Annamese* is the language spoken in Cochin-China, Annam, and Tongking. *Mon* is the same as the *Talieng* language, spoken in Pegu. *Khmer* is the usual philological name for the language of *Cambodja*. Dialects connected, and closely connected with these, are, however, spoken in India.

Malayan Peninsula was originally invaded *from the South*, at a time when probably the Indian Archipelago and Australia formed one immense continent.

In any case, as Messrs. Skeat and Blagden have taken considerable pains to prove, it is perfectly clear that in the Malay Peninsula we have *two* very clear types, as well as a *third* one, which is at present somewhat doubtful.

First, we have the *Semang* or *Negroid* type.

Secondly, we have the *Dravidian* type, shown in the *Sakai*.

Thirdly, we have the *Jakun* type, which has remained the *least* pure, but which shows in many points resemblance to the *Mongolian* type.* In how far this *Mongolian* type, can be considered as an *original* type is a " vexed question." From a linguistic point of view *Mongolian* as a language shows anything but originality, and is undoubtedly a *Misch-Sprache* (as the Germans call it) containing both *Turanian* and *Dravidian* elements.

In my opinion we have in the *Sakai* the pure *Dravidian* element, or better the so-called *Hamitic* element. Anyone who looks at the faces and the build of the *Sakai* as illustrated in the work of Messrs. Skeat and Blagden, must be struck by their resemblance to the *Gallas*, the *Somali*, and the *Southern Abyssinians ;* and if one studies the languages of the Gallas and the Somalis (for *Abyssinian* has been too much influenced by *Semitic* to allow a clear comparison) he must be immensely struck by the similarity of the roots of these languages and the roots of Sakai.†

The *Semang* is the *Negroid*, pure and simple. Unfortunately the term *Negroid* is a very badly chosen one, and its relation to the term *Negro* is liable to misconstruction, as if the former was a *kind of graft* upon the latter, a supposition which is absolutely at variance with the facts. I should propose to call the *Semang* a *Proto-Turanian*, i.e., the main element in that immense race, which we now call the *Turanians*, but which at present contains *Dravidian* and perhaps even *Aryan* elements. The term *Turanian*, indeed, is often given to all the *non-Aryan* languages of Asia, and seems to have been used by Max Müller in that sense. There is, however, a very great divergence between these languages, though Max Müller was undoubtedly right when he assumed " a genealogical

---

*There can scarcely be any doubt that the *Jakun* type, as at present existing in the Malacca Peninsula, has been strongly influenced by the *Malayan* element. Unfortunately nobody knows to-day what the *Malay* really is. Personally I am convinced that he is *not* indigenous to this part of Asia, and I am very much inclined to believe that he was of *Semitic* origin, and that he did not settle in these parts much before 1,500 B.C. In all probability he migrated from Southern Arabia, and is really a *Sabaean*.

†Although I carefully went into this matter, and have actually drawn up comparative lists, this subject cannot be treated in this essay, but must remain over to a future opportunity, if such should offer itself. *l'ita brevis—ars longa* must apply here.

relationship of all Turanian speech." It is, in my opinion, most likely that, at an early period, portions of the Semang or Sakai race went far north in Asia and Europe, but that, through the occurrence of the *second* glacial period, they were driven again south to more equatorial regions. Their long absence from the parent stock, the different environment and the influence of the colder climates, must have had considerable results, not only physical, but also linguistic; and perhaps this explains the divergence between the present Mon-Khmer group of languages and that generally called the Tibetan-Burman group. The people speaking these latter dialects certainly came from the North, as the most ancient legends show, but this *coming* may have been in reality a *returning*. The Khonds in India have a decided recollection of once having lived in the far north, beyond the Desert of Gobi.

That man existed upon earth with the Mammoth, the Cave-Lion, the hairy Rhinoceros, and the other animals which trod the northern earth between the *first* and the *second* glacial period, is a fact accepted at present by most geologists and anthropologists, although some difference of opinion exists about the placing of this period, and some scientists are inclined to accept only *one* glacial period.

The reason why I say that the great *Turanian* linguistic group contains at present even *Aryan* elements, is on account of the fact that in a large number of the *Northern Altaic* languages (as distinguished from the *Southern Altaic*, or *Bantu*) there are undoubted traces of Aryan; in some of the races which speak those languages there is even a strong Aryan element.

. In short, I may state that I should be inclined to defend, both upon ethnological and philological grounds, the following propositions.*

I. At a very early stage in the history of mankind the greater part of Further India was inhabited by a *Negroid* or *Proto-Turanian* race, which may have been aboriginals of this part, or may have moved thither from what is now the Indian Archipelago. At present we have not sufficient facts to enable us to determine the latter question.

II. At some time or other in gray antiquity—*i.e.*, many thousand years before Christ, and perhaps even in an earlier geological period of the earth—this part of Further India was

---

*It may be stated here that these propositions are by no means *new* or *startling*. *Quatrefages, De Morgan* and other learned men have held more or less the same views, though these have been violently combated by other scientists. The latest discoveries, to which I shall refer later on, do, however, show that *Quatrefages* especially had hold of the *right* end of the question, but that his views want careful testing.

invaded by another race of mankind, which we may call the *Hamitic.**

This later race caused a migration of the *Negroid* race, only a very small number of individuals remaining in Further India, and these are the ancestors of the present *Semang* in the Malacca Peninsula. The smallness of their number, and the fact that they were, no doubt, hunted from place to place by the newcomers, prevented the Semang from either increasing at an ordinary rate, or from making any material or intellectual progress. To-day the Semang belongs, with his relations, the Andamanians and Nicobarians, to the lowest races of man. In the Malay Peninsula several of the wildest tribes are still nomads, who do not stay longer than 3 or 4 days at one place, and the fact that this custom is ascribed to a command of the Deity, points to the conclusion that once upon a time it was absolutely necessary for their existence, that their enemies should not become acquainted with their hiding places. (Skeat and Blagden, I., p. 173, *note*).†

The *Negroid* race that left Further India after the invasion of the *Hamitic* race, wended its way westwards, and increasing in number, continually moved in sections to the west, so that it once upon a time formed the population of, at all events, the southern part of Europe. This has now been conclusively proved by the discovery of the so-called " Man of Grimaldi," who was found in Italy a short time ago by the Prince of Monaco. The skull of this man is of pure *Negroid* type, and very nearly approaches that of the present *Semang*.‡

But this Negroid race also invaded Africa, and here he changed into that sub-race which we now know as the *Hottentot Race*.

I am quite aware that this is a somewhat startling assertion, but there are a few proofs, which simply put the question beyond doubt. In the first place it is well known that the Hottentots are a *very* old race in Africa, and that in the very earliest time of historical Egypt they inhabited the land of

---

*I call this *another* race because at the time it invaded Further India it had clearly different characteristics from the *Negroid* races. But this fact does not really militate against the principle of *Unogenesis*, because it is quite possible that, at some remote time, the *two* races sprang from *one* source, but that they were compelled by natural circumstances and environment to follow different lines of development, which ultimately resulted in such variations, that they practically formed *two* races.

†In other races nomadic habits were developed by scarcity of food (*e.g.*, in the case of the Bushman in South Africa) ; in later cases, by the necessity of finding pasture for flocks (as is still done by several tribes in Central Asia). None of these causes could have operated in the Malay Peninsula, where both fruit trees, edible roots, and small game are, even to-day, very plentiful. Hence the agency must have been *human* here.

‡For particulars of this very important discovery I must refer my readers to an article by the renowned Dr. Verneau in *L'Anthropologie* of May, 1906, Vol. XVII., pts. 3–4, where the matter has been fully discussed. According to Dr. Verneau this negroid type is actually still traceable in some of the present inhabitants of Italy !

Punt. In 1533 B.C. an expedition (by no means the first) was sent by Queen Hatshepset to Punt, evidently the present Somaliland, and of this expedition we have a full account and several bas-reliefs, which will be found in Dr. E. A. W. Budge's " History of Egypt," vol. IV., pp. 5-11. The illustration on page 7 in this book shows the Hottentot with all his peculiarities, even to the *steatopygia*.*

This must settle the fact that the Hottentot is a " very old inhabitant " of Africa. But there is remarkable linguistic evidence to connect the Hottentot with the old *Negrito* of Further India. It is well known that the Hottentots called themselves *Khoi-Khoin*, which is a plural form, translated as *Men* or (wrongly) " men of men," the reduplication being simply the ancient form of the plural, found in many languages, even in Sumerian. Now in some Semang dialects *koin* is a man, and in Nicobarese *koinh*, or *koin*, is the usual name for *man* or *male*.

Although I have gone to considerable trouble in the matter, I have been unable to find any other languages besides the above, in which the word *koin* or *khoin* is used in the sense of " man," although related words are found in other languages of the Mon-Kmer group ; and this certainly shows that there must once upon a time have existed either a relation or an identity between the Hottentot and the Negroid of Further India.

But if one further carefully compares the language of the Semang and the language of the Hottentot, there is much in favour of the conclusion that once upon a time these languages were identical or nearly so. Naturally Hottentot has changed and has absorbed new elements in the 70 or 80 (or probably even more) centuries, since the Hottentots left the parent stock ; and the Semang and the Nicobarese have changed, though in a different direction. Not being yet in possession of any good work on Nicobarese or Andamese, I have not been able to devote much study to this interesting subject, but hope to do so soon, and will then publish my conclusions in a short form.† But the following few words are certainly remarkable in their close resemblance :—

‡*Hottentot*.		*Semang*.	
Kharob = bed.		Karob	= bed.
khora to stretch.		cherok	= to stretch.

---

*Skeat and Blagden in their aforequoted work, Vol. I., p. 578, mention a case of *steatopygia* in a *Semang* woman. It is a pity that this matter has not been treated more fully by the authors.

†An article on this question was published by me in the *African Monthly* of June, 1907, written since this essay was put in type.

‡For Hottentot I have principally made use of G. H. *Schils*' " Dictionnaire etymologique de la langue des Namas " (Louvain, 1895).

Hottentot.		Semang.	
khui	= to arise.	kyiu	= to arise.
sa	= to go.	cha	= to go.
tsa	= black.	sa-ya	= black.
ä	= to make a noise.	ä-eh	= to roar.
ä-rib (= a + ri) = dog.		ä-eh	= dog.
ä	= to drink.	añuh	= to drink.
ao	= to throw.	ä-uin	= to throw.
chä	= to burn.	chäm	= to light a fire.
chob	= cheek.	kaba	= cheek.
chob	= beard.	sabau	= beard.
dä	= to go.	däh	= to go.
do	= red.	to	= red.
di	= to play.	de	= to play.
ebe	= much.	ebeh	= much.
ga	= to speak.	cha	= to speak.
ga	= hard.	(te) ga	= hard.
gei-rab	= jackal.	chä-lau	= jackal
			(ch = g ; r = l).
ha (mo) = when?		ha (nadeh) = when?	

Even the clicks in Hottentot can be traced back in Semang. So if we represent the dental click by | we have the Hottentot | aob = snake agreeing with the Semang ekob, which was probably originally jkob or gkob ; Hottentot | awib = rain is the Nicobar ami = rain, originally gmi ; Hottentot | aro = to increase, find its correspondent form in Nicobar karu = to increase, which was probably ykaru in early times. As already said, I have not yet been able to give the subject that attention necessary to form a definite opinion, but from the little I have seen, I believe that the study of these two languages would lead to astonishing results.

It is well known that the Hottentots have some idea of a Divinity whom they call Tsuiguan or Tsuni-goan. Dr. T. Hahn has written a work upon this, which, however, contains most improbable theses, especially the idea that Tsuni-goam was a Solar God. The fact is that Tsuni-goam is the " Thunder God." His name still appears among the Ao-Nagas in India as Tsun-grem. This is clearly the Semang sion = spirit, and the Semang kaii or kare = thunder, which latter name in itself constitutes a God of a Semang tribe. (Compare the Semang form gumm = kaii.)*

---

*Masudi calls the God of the Zanj, Maklaudjalou, which probably meant in ancient Bantu " the Spirit of the Lightning." The Southern Bantu believe that the " Great Chief " has control over the lightning, and they never mourn over those who are killed by lightning, as they were " sent for " by the Great Chief.

At present this is all I can say in support of the theory, that the Semang who landed first in Africa, became there that race which we know as Hottentots.*

But the *whole* of the Negroid or Proto-Turanian race, which had left the Malacca Peninsula and Further India, did not wend its way westwards. A considerable number settled in the Indian Peninsula, now known to us as Hindostan.

Messrs. Skeat and Blagden have in a little map on page 442 of Vol. II. of their above-quoted work shown that the so-called Mon-Annam Family spread to India, and have rightly classed the Naga Territory as one of the places where languages related to the Semang and Sakai are spoken. But it would seem that the authors have put too narrow a limit upon the distribution of these languages.

An author of great repute, Mr. B. H. Hodgson, has shown that there exists an intimate relation between the languages spoken by the aborigines of North-Eastern India, and again between those languages on the one hand, and the Dravidian and Tibetan languages on the other hand.† An examination of the vocabularies of more than eighty Indian Non-Aryan languages, given by Hodgson, shows this relation very clearly.

Another great authority upon Anthropology, Professor Virchow, came to the conclusion that there existed even some ultimate relationship between the Veddas of Ceylon, the Tamil of South India and the Sakai, and though Virchow arrived at this conclusion upon purely anthropological grounds, it is certain that the results of linguistic researches carry him out.

We must therefore come to the conclusion that a considerable portion of the original Negroid or Proto-Turanian race settled in India, and that these *Semang* spread over a considerable part of that Peninsula. At a later period they were followed by the Hamitic race, the *Sakai*, who were perhaps then already mixed with a *Jakun* or Proto-Mongolian element. In India the Semang element became the *Kolarian*,

---

*I am leaving the real Negro tribes of Africa outside this essay, simply because otherwise my subject gets too vast to be treated in this essay. But I believe that the deeper we study the question, the more we must come to the conclusion that the lines between Negro and Bantu are far too sharply drawn at present, and that in reality it is very difficult to find the Borderland between these two. Naturally their languages have had an absolutely different development, just as the races had a completely different history.

†Hodgson's valuable work has been collected in two volumes, entitled "Miscellaneous Essays relating to Indian subjects," which form part of Trübner's Oriental Series. In some matter Hodgson perhaps goes too far, but there can scarcely be any doubt that in the main his views are correct, and deserve more notice than has been taken of them till now. Although I have by other works checked most of his vocabularies, I must here state that without his labours as a guide, I could scarcely have brought mine to a successful issue. Another valuable little work is Forbes' "Comparative Grammar of the Languages of Further India" (Allen & Co.: London, 1881).

and the Sakai-Jakun developed into the true *Dravidian*. But the races became mixed in many instances, and tribes arose which contained both elements. The most important of these tribes were undoubtedly those, of whom we find the remnants in that part of the population of India now known as the *Nagas*, and who principally inhabit that hilly country of the Central Provinces, known as *Nagpur*. To these *Nagas* I shall have to refer somewhat later at considerable length, for there cannot be the slightest doubt, but *the ancient Nagas are the direct ancestors of the first Bantu invaders of South Africa,*

I shall now adduce direct linguistic evidence in support of this assertion, and in doing so I shall not only make use of the principal *Naga-languages* in their *present* form, but also of many of the other Non-Aryan languages of India. For in the ancient times when the Bantu departed from India the differences between the dialects of the various aboriginal tribes inhabiting India were not as clear-cut as at present, and it is evident that elements not now found among the Naga-languages, but in the more or less related languages, must have formed part of the parent stem, and were thus introduced into ancient Bantu. Practically, the list that I am drawing up in the following pages, is the result of a comparison of about sixty African languages with more than eighty Indian dialects. It has, I need scarcely say, entailed an immense amount of work, but I considered it advisable, under the circumstances, to travel over as wide a range as possible, so as to be certain of the results. On the other hand the limits of this essay have compelled me to keep the list within certain bounds. Hence I only give here twelve words, but these are surely enough for practical purposes.

In drawing up these lists I have, as far as possible, traced the words back to their *Semang* or *Sakai* originals. The fact that this could not be done in *all* cases, is principally due to want of material. The only list of *Sakai* and *Semang* words at my disposal was that found as an appendix to Skeat and Blagden's "Pagan Races of the Malay Peninsula," which, though fairly full, is by no means complete. Unfortunately, I was unable to obtain either a Andamese or a Nicobarese dictionary. As regards the Indian languages, I have principally made use of Hodgson's Comparative Vocabularies, and of a small number of other Vocabularies and Dictionaries, which I was able to obtain with the limited means at my disposal.

Where I considered explanations or remarks necessary I have done so in a separate column, in which I have also shown the related words in North-Altaic.

COMPARATIVE LIST OF WORDS IN BANTU AND IN NON-ARYAN LANGUAGES OF INDIA.

English.	Bantu.	Languages of India.	Malacca Languages.	Remarks.
Air .. (1)	Zulu umoya Kafir umoya Mang'anja mpweya Herero oru-muinyo Shuna nueya	Sak. mwiyahe Ceylon Malabar ayayam	Sakai gemuyong = wind Semang begiyu = wind	The words are arranged according to the corresponding roots in *Semang* and *Sakai*, thus giving a clear view of the development of the Indian languages from these, and of the Bantu languages from the latter. In some cases, however, the Indian languages seem to have lost some of the roots, and then the Bantu is referred immediately to the Malacca roots.
(2)	Secwana phehi Suaheli upepo Luganda empewo Wisa impepo Senga mpepo	Khassi phuh = to blow Padi phusa = air Chouras'ya phu-rim = air Ao Naga mo-pung = wind	Sakai puh = to blow Sakai pää = air	Compare the following words from the *Ugro-Altaic group* :—
(3)	Suaheli hewa	Sindbhum Kol hoiyo Sontal hoye Rodong liyu Vaju hojum	Sakai hawa Sakai (ko)-hoi = breath	Mandchu niye-cecun = air (4). Finnish henki = breath (3). Japanese nari = air (4). iki = breath (3) (k = h). mawaru = wind (1). piheges = breathing (2). Magyar hewa = air (3). Turkish (ne) fess = air (2) (f = p). Sumerian mer = wind (1). Votian kvaz = air (3) (k = h).
(4)	Isubu ngoi, ngo Suaheli anga		Sakai nya = to blow	

English.	Bantu.		Languages of India.	Malacca Languages.		Remarks.
2. Arrow (1)	Mpongwe / Oshikuanjama / Umbundu / Kinjamuesi / Kongo	ozanga ohengo usongo issonga nzanga	Mithan Naga / Nowgong Naga / Ao Naga — san la-sang i-zang	{ Sakai / Semang	rong sen (loi)	(a) The Zulu word is a compound of two words meaning the same, a not uncommon occurrence in Eastern languages.
(2)	Kafir	(u)tolo	Angami Naga — tilösi	Semang / (Andamese)	tela tola	(b) The second word in the Dualla expression *dipunga* means "bow," just like the *loi* in Semang *sen-loi*.
(3)	Suaheli / Luganda / Herero	mshale akasale (omu)zi	Uraon / Sinbhum Kol — char sarh	Sakai	segar = arrow	(c) The Semang and Sakai principally use the ⁄ *the* as *an*, and the use of " bw and arr o " *ably* came into use after *their* arrival in *this*. Most of the words given here as " arrow," really mean the " dart of the blowpipe." For that reason not many equivalents are found in the Ugro-Altaic languages.
(4)	Duala mlanya (dipunga)		Kondh — pinju			
(5)	Mang'anja / Kikuya / Aduma / Shambala	mu-lwi nu-gui bota mu-vi	Radong / Nachhereng / Toda — lhe he'i a-bu	Sakai	bel	Compare, however,
(6)	Zulu	umcibityolo	Sangpang / Anga Maga — cebi tilösi			Turkish tir (2) (r=l) / selim (1)

Arm	Bantu.	Language o nd		Malacca anguages.	Remarks
(1)	Zulu umkono	B do na:	**ha**-ti	Sekai kan-grı	(1) From the roots it **would** thus seem that the arm is the "catch-holder," or the "taker," and that will explain the fact why in so many languages the **same** for *hand* and *arm* are **held**.
	Mang'anja mkono	Tamil kai	= to take	Semang chas	
	ı **Ali** mkono	Lepcha ka	= to take	Sakai (pô)gan = to **take** hold	
	Kamba mokono	Lhota Naga hansi	= to take	Sakai kom = to **take**	
	Luganda omukono	Kuling'ya khau	= to take		
	Tsnbu **nko**	Uraon hona	= to take	(Khmer kan = to take)	
	Kiwywamesi ku **duo** mkono	I **mehhong** ko	= to take		Compare.—
		Chentsu ko	= to take		Finnish kangon = arm (1).
					Turkish kol = arm (2).
					Syrjenian ki = arm (1).
					kin = **and** (1).
					chub = to take hold (1).
					kar = **and** (1).
					Cagataish 1 ar = arm (1).
					Magyar **drok** = arm (1).
(2)	Kafır ingala	Bahing gu		Sakai (pe)gak = to hold	Magyar fogui = to catch hold of (3) (b = f)
	Tebele ingalo	Vayu got			
	Suaheli guba	Kashmirian gul			
	Aduma ghogo				
(3)	Bobangi loboko	Angami Naga bu		Semang be(lang)	
	Ronga ahoko	Tamil bujam			
		Thaksy'a bhakau = to take			

English.	Bantu.	Languages of India.	Malacca Languages.	Remarks.

4. And .. (1)	Zulu na
	Kafir ne
	Mang'anja ni
	Herero na
	Mpongwe ni, na
	Suaheli na
	Kamba na
	Kikuya na
	Luganda na
	Tsuba na
	Wisa na
	Aduna na
	Ronga na
	Senga na
	Shambala na
	Kinynamesi na
		Lhota Naga na
		Telugu nni
		Tuhvu no
			Sakai nan = more, yet, still, and	(1) Luganda *era* is connected with *lü*, with the ordinary change of *l* into *r*.
				
				Compare:—
				  Finnish ja = and (3).
				  Votian no = ,, (1).
				  Turkish ve = ,, (3) (v = y).

(2)	Secwana le Tebele la Umbundu la	Lambiehhong la	Sakai lü = also, and	
(3)	Kongo ye	Ao Naga ya Chentsu ye	Semang yan = remainder	

h.	Bird	Bantu.	Languages of India.	Malacca	Remarks.
(1)	Bird	Zulu — inyoni Secwana — nonyane Mpongwe — nyani Kongo — nuni Kamba — nyunui Kikuya — nyoni Luganda — enyonyi Dualla — enun	Chepang — moa Thaksya — nomya Yakha — nua Lambiehhong — nowa	Semang — ma-nu = fowl	1. *Manu* is the common word in many Eastern languages for "fowl" or "bird." The root of the word is evidently *nu*, and the *ma* in Semang is an older prefix. In Tibetan *nya* means "the eggborn," and this is evidently the idea underlying the word for "bird."
(2)		Kafir — intaka		Nicobarese — ta-fuk = fowl	Compare:— Sirjenian kai = bird (3). Turkish kush = bird (3). Finnish kana = fowl (3). Magyar tynk = fowl (2). „ madar = bird (4). Sumerian chu = bird (3).
(3)		Wisa — ichuni Senga — chuni	Dadhi — chari Sontal — chene Bhurnij — chene	Sakai — chem = bird	
(4)		Herero — ondera Suaheli — ndege Shambala — ndege	Angami Naga — peri (p = d)	Sakai — dena = jungle fowl	

English.	Bantu.	Languages of India.	Malacca Languages.	Remarks.
To drink (1)	Zulu puza Tebele puza	Dadhi pyu Pakhya piu	Semang (ma)bu	Compare:—
(2)	Herero nua Suaheli nywa Oshindonga nua Kongo nua Luganda nywa Tsubu nyō Aduma egnua Bobangi nua Dualla nyó Seewana mwa Mang'anja mwa	Brahma nga Kami nei Toung-lhoe nwa	Sakai nyo; ŋun	Magyar inni = to drink (2). Finnish imea = „ „ (2). „ juoda = „ „ (3). Japanese nomu = „ „ (2). Votian juny = „ „ (3). Manchu omimbi = „ „ (2). Sumerian nag = „ „ (2).
(3) Mpongwe	jonga	Ao Naga a-yong Namsang Naga joko	Semang yam	

		Bantu.	Languages of India	Malacca Languages.	Remarks.
To go	(1)	Zulu ya Kafir ya Oshindonga jo Wisa ija Oshikuanyama ja Senga ya	Denwar ya = to come Sepcha yiu = to go Khasi jia	Semang ya = to bring Semang ya chöp = to go	1. The ideas "to come," "to go" and "to bring" are mixed up in most ancient languages, and can often be referred to the same root. This has caused considerable confusion in the form of the respective expressions, and these are often difficult to follow up. Besides the roots here treated, there are several others which have made their influence felt in Bantu as well as in the Indian languages. Thus the Isubu *timba* = to go, finds its counterpart in Lepcha *ti* = to come, and this again in Sakai *tiba* = to arrive.
	(2)	Zulu hamba Kafir hamba Ronga famba		Semang hambin = to bring	
	(3)	Mang'anja choka		Sakai chok = to go	

	(4)	Herero yenda
		Suaheli enda
		Luganda genda
		Tsubu kende
		Aduna eyende
		Shuna enda
			Brahmu yenga	Semang jeng = to bring	Compare:—
					Finnish käyda. = to go (4)?
					Turkish ghelmek = to come (3)
					Magyar gyak = to go (3).
					  „ joni = to come (4).
					Japanese chaku = to come (3).
					  „ juku = to go (1).

	(5)	Manga'nja pita Secwana potologa Suaheli potea Wisa puta Senga pita	Bahing'gya' pito = to bring	Semang pätäp = to bring	

English.	Bantu.	Languages of India.	Malacca Languages.	Remarks.
8. Fire .. (1)	Zulu umlilo Kafir umlilo Secwana molelo Herero omu-riro Luganda omu-lira Wisa omu-lilo Senga mu-lilo	Lhota omi = flame Angami Naga le = heat, hot Sontal loloa = hot Sinbhum Kol lolo = hot	Semang (k)lil = to twist, to twirl	(1) The Bantu words of No. 1 are probably compounds, from *omi* and *lil*. This would bring the origin of the words back to the fact that originally fire was obtained by the twirling of one piece of wood upon another. The very common root-word *mi* = fire, seems to have been lost in the present Malacca languages.
(2)	Suaheli moto Mang'anja moto	Angami Naga mitu = flame	Semang metut = to burn	(2) Dualla *wea*, Isubu *wea* and Bobangi *meya* may be connected with ancient Tamil *veyya* = hot, but I have been unable to trace any Malacca form for this word.
(3)	Kongo tiya ,, tuvia	Irala tu Malayalim tiyya Tuluvu tu	Sakai tot = fire ,, teki = to scorch	Compare:—
(4)	Aduma mbua Kikuya mwaki Dualla wea	Kumi bi = hot	Sakai bɔt = hot	Japanese honɔ = flame (6). Turkish atesh = fire (3). Magyar tüz = ,, (3). Finnish tuli = ,, (3). Sirjenian bi = ,, (4). Sumerian ki-ne = ,, (6).
(5)	Oshindonga etanga	Savara togo = fire	Sakai anggu = charcoal	
(6)	Mpongwe ogom Kamba iko	Dungmali ku = hot	Semang ongoyd = to burn	

English.	Bantu.	Languages of India.	Malacca Languages.	α	Remarks.
Blood .. (1)	Zulu igazi Kafr igazi Mang'anja mwazi Tebele igazi	Thaksya ka Bahing'gya husi Nowgong Naga azu Rajmahali kezu Ao Naga azu	Semang gas = life		(1) The ideas of "life" and "blood" are nearly connected in all ancient languages. Ka is a very old word for "soul", or "life," as is proved by the Egyptian ka = the soul.
(2)	Secwana madi Isubu makai Kongo manga Dualla maiya	Sinbhum Kol myun Sontal mayam Savara miyamu	Semang mahum = life, blood		(2) The form chaku found in Mon. seems to have been lost in the Malacca group. Skeat and Blagden connect it with Sakai ĕ-kur = body, but this is very doubtful.
(3)	Luganda omu-sai	Singpho sai	Sakai zaɩs = life, blood		Compare :—
					Finnish suku = blood (4).
					Turkish kan = „ (1).
(4)	Kikuya sakamo Shambala sakame		Mon. chaku = life, body		Japanese ketsu = „ (1) (ts = z).
					Magyar ĕlet = life (6).
					Sumerian muda = blood (2).
(5)	Aduma likila		Sakai luka = wound		
(6)	Wisa omulopa Bobangi malongo Kilolo balongo Senga mlopa	Kocch lohu Tharu lohu Khamti lit Chentsu lahu	Sakai lĭt, lŏd = blood		

English.	Bantu.	Languages of India.	Malacca Languages.	Remarks.
10. Cat .. (1)	Mang'anja mpaka Secwana phage Suaheli paka Kamba mbaka Kikuye nempaka Wisa mpaka	Talien pak-way Kocch bag = tiger Kiswar baghi = ,, Pakhya baghi = ,,	Semang baling = tiger	(1) It is probable that in Further India the Malacca races were not acquainted with the domestic cat, but only with the tiger and the tiger-cat, and it is but natural that when they became acquainted with the domestic cat, they transferred the name of its larger brother to it.
(2)	Mpongwe pus	Chingtangya pusu Sontal pusi Tuluvu puchche	Semang kuching Sakai ku-ching	(2) In (2) we apparently have the usual interchange between k and p. Compare:— Turkish kedi = cat (3). ,, bubr = tiger (1). Finnish kissa = cat (2). Magyar macska = ,, (1). Sirjenian kan = ,, (3). Votian kusin = ,, (2).
(3)	Dualla singi Shambala chonjwe Senga chona Kafir ingada	Mithan Naga chianu Khari Naga a-khu Brahmn sya Dadhi gai	Semang chiai = tiger	

			Languages of India.	Malacca Languages.	Remarks.
1. Head	(1)	Mang'anja mutu Oshindonga omutsue Kongo ntu Kamba mutue Luganda omutwe Wisa umutwe Aduma mutchue Bobangi mutu Senga mutu Shambala mutwi	Kocch mura Dadhi mud Thari mudi Abor Miri mittuk = above Lohorung miltu = ,, Bahali muttu = ,, Tuluvu nett = ,,	Sakai meta = above	It may be that the Bantu *mutu* is derived from an old word *tu* or *tui* meaning "head," in some Eastern dialects, with the prefix *mu*, but I can scarcely accept this in view of the Indian forms. The idea of "above," that is "what is on the top," seems to agree better with the Indian equivalents of the two expressions. Though it may seem tempting to connect *mutu* = head, with *mutu* = man, I am convinced that the two words have, etymologically, nothing in common. (Compare:— Japanese tsu-muri = head (1). ,, kubi = ,, (2). Magyar fö = ,, (3) (f = b). ,, fö = above.* Finnish pää = head (3). ,, kallo = ,, (2). Turkish bash = ,, (3).
	(2)	Suaheli nkuu Haussa kai	Shoto Naga kuur	Semang kai	
	(3)	Mponge ewonjo	Thling'gya bui Sinbhum Kol bu	Sakai buj (w = b)	* This seems to carry out the correctness of the etymology of (1), as given by me.

English.	Bantu.	Languages of India.	Malacca Languages.	Remarks.
12. Mouth (1)	Zulu — umlomo Kafir — umlomo Secwana — molomo Kamba — moomo Kikuya — miromo Isubu — molumbi Shuna — nromo	Denwar — mu-lun	Sakai — mulo	(1) In Bantu we have in (1) apparently a metathesis of syllable *lomo* for *mulo*, a phenomenon by no means uncommon in these groups. In Kamba the *l* has been dropped. Compare:— Magyar nyilas = mouth (3). Japanese kuchi = ,, (2). Turkish dihan = ,, (2)? ,, kapi = opening (2). Sumerian ka = mouth (2).
(2)	Mang'anja — kamwa Suaheli — kanwa Oshindonga — okana Mpongwe — ogwana Luganda — akanwa Wisa — akanwa	Lepcha — ka Khasi — khnium	Semang kann = to keep in the mouth	
(3)	Herero — otyi-nyo Kongo — nua Bobangi — munya Aduma — mugnua	Dhinal — mui Kachcha Naga — mimui	Sakai nyak, nyag, minyun, nyui } = mouth	

SECTION VII.

Thus far I have established *prima facie* evidence of the fact that originally the Bantu came from Further India, but that the two races, the *Sakai* and *Semang*, having amalgamated to a certain extent, there arose a new race, the *Ugro-Altaic* or *Turano-Hamitic* (as it really should be called) and that the Bantu form the *southern* branch of that race. That is, at all events, the clear tendency of the *linguistic* evidence brought forward by me.

There is *other* evidence in favour of this theory, and fairly strong evidence, but I must leave the consideration thereof to a later stage of this work. Not to disturb the *philological* context of this essay, I must now first discuss the question of the second Bantu invasion, which, as I said, I consider to have come from the mouths of the Tigris and Euphrates.

I have in the first list, Nos. 27-70, given a considerable number of Sumerian words, which seem to be immediately connected with Bantu expressions having the same meaning. In the comparative list of Bantu, Indian and Malacca languages, it will be, however, seen that *Sumerian*, as an Ugro-Altaic language, is derived from the same original stock as Bantu. It might thus be argued that the Sumerian and the Bantu words are similar, merely on account of having a *common origin*. But there are certain facts which show that the connection between *Sumerian* and *Bantu* must have been *more* close and *more* direct, than would have been the case if only influences of *common origin* had been at work.

History teaches us that the various Sumerian and Accadian communities were conquered at a fairly early date by a Semitic race, which is known as the Babylonians. This Semitic race adopted, to a large extent, the civilisation of the conquered, which was certainly higher than their own, and, among other things, took over the Sumerian form of writing known as the *Cuneiform* or *Wedge-writing*. This latter fact seems to have been of considerable influence upon the Semitic language of the Babylonians, as well as upon the Sumerian language itself, which latter took over Semitic words in its vocabulary.* In the course of time the old Babylonian Empire came under the influence of the later Assyrian kingdom, which was also of Semitic origin, and gradually there seems to have collected near the mouths of the Tigris and Euphrates a somewhat mixed population, known in Assyrian history as the " men of the sea lands." These people probably spoke a Sumerian dialect, strongly interspersed with Semitic, not only Babylonian, but also Southern Arabic.

*That this is a fact is well known to all students of Assyrian and Sumerian, but the principle has certainly been carried too far in *J. D. Prince's* " Materials for a Sumerian Lexicon " (Leipzig, 1906). This is due to the fact that Prince has not grasped the idea that both in Sumerian and in Semitic we have a strong Turanian element.

There is, as every Bantu scholar knows, a very strong Semitic element in several of the Bantu languages, and a strong Semitic physical element, which cannot be of purely Arabian origin, is very noticeable in some of the Bantu tribes living in the neighbourhood of the River Niger in West Africa.

From a philological point of view, the Semitic influence upon Bantu can partly be traced to Arabic, and this is particularly noticeable in Suaheli. This Arabic element is, to a very large extent, of later origin, and is probably due to the fact that since the 8th century after Christ large Arabian colonies and kingdoms were established along the East Coast of Africa, from Cape Guardafui to Cape Delgado. These Arabian kingdoms remained in existence till far in the 17th century, and even to this day, this Arabian element makes itself felt through the commerce which Arabians carry on not only along the coast of Africa, but also in the very centre of the Continent.

There is, however, another and older Semitic element in some Bantu languages, which cannot be referred to Arabic and which, I am convinced, is of Assyrian origin. The most striking instance of this is found in the *Shuna* language, spoken by the Mashonas* or, as they call themselves, the *Makalanga*. A very fair dictionary of this *Shuna* language has been published by Mr. W. A. Elliot, of the London Missionary Society, entitled " Dictionary of the Tebele and Shuna Languages " (London, 1897), of which I have made use.

The following short comparative list will show how strong a relation apparently exists between the Assyrian and the Shuna language, and in some instances the relationship is so remarkable as to make a direct Assyrian influence, as it were, a *sine qua non*.

Shuna.		*Assyrian.*	
1. pishana	= a severe pain.	pishannu	= to cause trouble.
2. dzudzura	= to paint.	zurah	= to shine.
		(as causative, " to make shining.")	
3. sima	= to plant.	simnu	= a plant.

---

*The name *Mashona* has been objected to by several scientists, who prefer to call the tribe the *Makalanga*. This latter name is supposed to mean " the People of the Sun," *Ma* = people, *ka* = of, *langa* (for *ilanga*) = sun. I strongly doubt whether this is not a case of Bantu popular etymology. As far as I am aware, the preposition *of* in Bantu does not enter into any *tribal* name of the Bantu. The *Makalanga* are probably an offshoot of another tribe found more north, and called the *Makaranga* (*r* = *l*), and this makes me inclined to think that the real meaning is " the people of Karan," which might have quite another explanation. Why the term *Mashona* should be objected to, I cannot quite see. The expression means " the people who hiss." a name which was probably given them by some other Bantu tribe, on account of the large amount of *sh* and other sibilants in the Shuna language, a factor which certainly distinguishes Shuna from other Bantu languages.

	Shuna.			*Assyrian.*	
4.	msimba	=power.	sibu	=to grasp firmly.
5.	bisu	=to produce.	basu	=to be.
				(as causative, " to produce.")
6.	zwara	=to propagate.	zaru	=to propagate.
7.	roba	=to punish.	ra'abu	=to be angry.
8.	idanga	=a cattle kraal.	dunnu	=a bed (really " a place to rest in ").
9.	shinga	=to labour.	sakanu	=to work, make.
10.	bona	=to look.	baru	=to see.

(N.B.—Semitic *r* generally changes in Bantu into *n*, as most Bantu languages have not the true *r*.)

11.	penga	=to be mad.	pinga	=to be mad ?*
12.	igona	=plank.	kannu	=plank ?†
13.	igondoro	=goatram.	gadu	=ram.
14.	nzhira	=road.	girru	=road.

(The Assyrian guttural is here softened in Shuna into a sibilant, a common occurrence.)

15.	berenga	=to read.	beru	=sight.
	(*Tebele* bala =to read.)		baru	=to see.*
16.	pira	=to sacrifice.	pirketi	= a kind of sacrifice.
17.	ishangu	=shoe.	senu	=shoe.

*Delitzsch gives in his Assyrian " Handwörterbuch," p. 532, the word *pinga* without any translation, but it seems to me from the context of IV. R. 8, that the translation " to be mad," would fit in very well. If this be correct, we have here an instance of the Shuna language enabling us to find the meaning of an Assyrian word, and I believe we might meet with more cases of a similar nature.

†Delitzsch does not translate this word, but the meaning " plank " would seem to fit in, though in one extract quoted by him it might have the related meaning of " sheet (of iron)." The Sumerian *is-gan-sa-kak* would certainly support the translation " plank." Compare *is-gu-surgasuru* = beam (Japanese *kosen* =" beam," Sirjenian *gozna* = beam).

*These words, which, as far as I am aware, are not found in any other Bantu language, must be very old, as the later Bantu lost the art of reading probably soon after his arrival in Africa. But in Sumir and Babylonia nearly every one could read, as we know from Hilprechts' " Explorations in Biblelands." For this reason I venture to connect the Bantu words with the Assyrian *beru* and *baru*. I may state that it seems to me that even in some Assyrian texts *baru* may have the meaning of " to read." The ideas of " seeing " and " reading " are nearly related, and we often find mention made of inscriptions placed in such a manner " that the people could see them ' (*i.e.* " read them ").

18. gu-ipa   = sin.   egu   = to sin.

19. dakwane   = small.   dakku   = small.

20. nzimbha   = tsetse fly.   zumbu   = fly.

21. imanda   = anger.   mammu   = anger.

22. dabira   = to answer.   gabru   = to answer.

(N.B.—The change from *g* to *d* is certainly very remarkable in this case.)

23. musana   = back.   seru   = back.

24. ba   = to be.   basu   = to be.

25. naku   = to be beautiful. nasku   = to be beautiful.

26. ishiri   = bird.   ishshuru = bird.

27. kondamu = to bow.   kadadu   = to bow.

28. mpeto   = border.   patu   = border.

29. mñwana (*pl. bana*) = child. banu   = child.

(N.B.—The Shuna singular is a contraction of *mun-wana*, where the *w* is the regular representative of the *b*.)

30. buya   = to come.   ba'u   = to come.

31. tebera   = to come after. tibu   = to come after.

32. idama   = a command.   adu   = a command.

33. shandura = to change.   shanu   = to change.

34. buraya   = to destroy.   balu   = to destroy.

35. zwimba   = to desire.   shabu   = to desire.

36. buruka   = to descend.   buru   = descendant. .

37. imauri   = a deaf man. amiru   = deaf.

38. sweta   = to draw.   shatu   = to draw.

39. simiga   = to fix.   samu   = to fix.

40. erera   = to flow.   gararu   = to flow.

(The initial *g* has dropped in Bantu, and the Shuna has really reverted to the older Indian form, as is clear from the Dravidian *aru* = river).

41. paradziga	= to fly (of sparks).	parashu	= to fly.
42. nganu	= garden boun-[dary.	gannatu	= garden boundary.
43. ishaba	= eland.	shabitu	= gazelle.
44. teberana	= to go, in Indian file.	tibu	= to go.
45. bimba	= to be happy.	bennu	= happiness.
46. tjera	= to make a hole.	churru	= hole.
47. shaba	= to hunt.	shadu	= to hunt.
48. pfiga	= to lock.	pichu .	= to lock.
49. sungira	= to lock.	shigaru	= to lock.
50. da	= to love.	dadu	= love (n).
51. paradzanu	= to part.	parasu	= to part.
52. shaya	= to want.	shugu	= want (n).
53. sura	= to break wind	saru	= wind.
54. idzese	= wood.	issu	= wood.
55. mu-ali	= god.	ilu	= god.

(Perhaps this is one of the strongest proofs concerning the relationship of Shuna and Assyrian. If the word was the only Semitic word in the first-named language, one might feel inclined to ascribe it to Arabic influence, but in this case this can scarcely be done, even admitting that, at a certain time in their history, the Mashonas came into close contact with the Arabians, which is highly probable. But except in a few tribes who have turned Mahomedan, the word *Allah*, for God, is nowhere found in Bantu dialects, and even Suaheli, which shows very marked influences of Arabic in its vocabulary, has retained the word *Muunti* for the Deity. Under such circumstances, and taking into consideration the other evidences regarding the relation of the two languages, I am convinced that *Mu-ali* must be referred to Assyrian origin).

56. Shuna *she* = ruler.   Assyrian *sha* = lord, master.

Delitzsch is of opinion that the Assyrian word is really an adaptation of the third personal pronoun = *he*, but I am not so sure of this, and both words might be referred to Semang *edjah* = chief, the Assyrian having adopted the word from the Sumerian. But in any case the Shuna seems to be the only Bantu language which has taken the word over, unless Dualla *sanga* = " father, master," must be referred to the same root, which is very doubtful.

57. Shuna *msafuri* = copper. Assyrian siparru = copper.

The Shuna form is here really the older, and the history of the word is so remarkable and interesting that I shall give here a short account of it. The original word for " copper " was *chu-phar*, a Turanian word, meaning " beyond the sea," or " from the other side of the sea," from Turanian *chu* = water, sea, and *phar* = beyond. This name was probably given to it by the Turanian tribes of Western Asia, because they obtained their copper from India across the sea. The Sumerians called it *ud-ka-bar*, *i.e.*, " the metal from beyond the sea," *ka-bar* being the equivalent of the original *chu-phar*, with this difference that in ancient Turanian the *ch* was soft, and the word was pronounced *su-p-har*, the *ph* being a real aspirated *p*. In this way *two* words for copper arose, one with the soft *ch* and the other with the hard *ch* or *k*. The Semites followed the soft pronunciation, and hence we have in Assyrian *siparru*, in Arabian *asfar* (brass), etc. ; and this pronunciation was carried over by the Sumero-Babylonians to the Bantu, when the language of the former had already absorbed considerable Semitic elements.

But the *ancient* Sumerians (before coming into contact with the Semites) went over to the island of Cyprus, under the leadership of their great conqueror, Sargon I., who ruled about 3700 B.C. In all probability they formed a settlement on the island, a fact which is patent from the old Sumerian and Babylonian cylinders and seals found on that island. They found rich copper mines on the island, and called it *kabar* or *ku-par*, and hence the Greeks, when they became acquainted with the island, called it *kupross*, whence our name " copper " for the metal in question. So it happens that to-day we call it " copper " and the Shuna call it *msafura*, a slightly changed form of *sipparu*, and up till now there probably was neither an Englishman nor a Mashona who was aware that in reality they are using the same word under different aspects of phonology.

To prove how correct this explanation is I may point to Arabian *nuhas* and Hebrew *nehast*, both meaning " copper.' Both these words are derived from the Indian *Nagas*, the name of the people who brought the copper from India to Western Asia, and who, as I shall show, were the ancient Ugro-Altaic

traders, who lived near the mouth of the Indus. This is shown .
by the Ethiopian *nahas* = copper, and as in that language *g*
and *h* interchange, there is every probability that the old word
for copper was *nagas*.

There may be some people who are sure to stamp this kind
of thing *Philological Romance*, but these should not forget
that often "*facts* are stranger than *fiction*."

Some of the ancient Assyrian words were taken over in
Bantu with *metathesis of syllables*. So :

Shuna.	Assyrian.
tjero = ghost.	ru-chu = ghost.
tizha = to run away.	satu = to run away.
ma-kusero = skin scrapings.	karasu = to skin.
di-muga = to be sorry.	agamu = to be sorry.

There is, besides this apparently direct connection between
many words in Shuna and Assyrian, a good deal more evidence
of Assyrian influence upon Bantu, especially in that branch
of Bantu which we call the *Bechuana*. For instance, there
was a chief among the Barolong called *Tau* = the lion,
and we have also the tribe of the Ba-taung (= the
people of the place of the lion). But *Tau* is nothing
else but the Assyrian *tau* = to eat, and we have thus here the
lion called "the eater," a name he also had in Semitic, as is
clear from Judges 15 : 14. "Out of the eater (*i.e.*, the lion)
came forth meat." (See *Fürst*, Hebrew Dictionary, *sub voce*
akal = to eat.)

So the name of the South African supposed desert known
to us as the *Kalihari*, is nothing else but the somewhat changed
compound of Assyrian *kalu* = " all," and *harbu* (Sumerian
aria) = " desert," and may thus suitably be translated as
" great desert."

In the other Southern Bantu tribes there are undoubtedly
several words connected with Assyrian. Zulu *baba* = to burn,
seems to agree with Assyrian *kababu* = to burn, and Zulu *zi* =
kraal, with Assyrian *zirru* = fence. But there are *two* words
in Southern Bantu which are without the slightest doubt of
Sumerian and Assyrian origin.

The first is *unkulukulu*, the name given by the Zulus and
Kafirs to a being, which was apparently a high deity, but of
which the Bantu have not any more a clear conception. Bishop
Callaway has in vain tried to get at the bottom of this matter,
but he could not get further than the idea of " the great-great-
one," or " the old-old one," which the Bantu themselves at
present possess of this mysterious being, and who they even
believe to have been a *man* once upon a time. Authorities
like Callaway and Max Müller have therefore come to the
conclusion that we have here to do with a case of " ancestor-
worship." But if the Zulu were able to remember his ancestral

home, he would have no difficulty in connecting *Unkulukulu* with the old Sumerian *An-gal-gal*, the Great God of Heaven, with which it agrees letter for letter. *Gal* in Sumerian means " great," and is exactly the same word as Zulu *kulu*, which in some of the Bantu dialects, *c.g.*, Secwana is *golo*. The repetition merely gives emphasis to the adjective. *An* in Sumerian meant " the God of Heaven," and in Zulu would become *un*, the *u* being, so to say, the " leading vowel " in Southern Bantu and often taking the place of an original *a*. By such a very simple process of Comparative Philology we are able to settle a matter which has considerably troubled missionaries as well as Bantu scholars, including the great Dr. Bleek himself.

The *second* word I wish to refer to here, is the well-known *ama-pakati*. In Zulu and Kahr this word denotes the councillors of the chief, and the word is generally explained as meaning the " middle-men," from the adverb *pakati* = middle. These *ama-pakati* are, in a certain sense, the sub-chiefs of the districts in which they reside, and there represent the great .chief. It is their duty to watch over the behaviour of the people, and to hear minor cases ; to collect the fines imposed upon evildoers ; and they are also responsible for the due payments of the " presents," to which the tribal. chief is entitled, and as these " presents " are really a mere euphonism for " taxes " they may be said to be the chief tax-collectors.

In Assyrian, *pahatu* (*pachatu*) meant a district or division of the kingdom, and the governors or satraps who ruled these divisions in the name of the king were called the *Amel-pachati*, which is, letter for letter, the same as the Bantu *ama-pakati*.* Delitzsch derives this word from the verb *pichu*, which means " to impose taxes, to rule," and this is probably correct. It is therefore likely that the adverb *pakati* = middle, is derived from the noun, and not *vice-versa*, and this is more probable, because in Bantu most adverbial expressions are really special forms of nouns.

Considering therefore the presence of a distinct *Assyrian*, or rather *Babylonian* element in several Bantu dialects, we are entitled to come to the conclusion that the Sumerian-Babylonian influence on Bantu must have proceeded *directly* from the mouths of the Tigris and Euphrates, and that by means of an immigration from that part of Asia.†

---

*There exists in Assyrian a parallel form with *k*, viz., *pakadu*. with a primary meaning " to protect," and a secondary meaning of " to rule, to govern."

†I am using the phrase " the *mouths* of the Tigris and Euphrates " purposely, because in ancient times the two rivers had their separate embouchures, and did not join, at as present, in the *Schatt-el-Arab*. The waters of the Persian Gulf are constantly receding and it has been calculated that in 6,000 years the land at the mouth of these rivers has gained more than 150 miles upon the sea.

SECTION VIII.

We shall now consider some other evidences regarding the Origin of the Bantu, for, as has been said " the relations between races of mankind cannot be determined by philology alone." This is a truism which anthropologists are continually impressing upon philologists, and in a measure they are correct in doing so. Anthropology, however, would no doubt attempt to settle the question by the shape, capacity, etc., of the skull, a question I am not going to enter upon, because I know too little upon the subject. But it is to be hoped that some competent authority will soon take this matter up, upon the lines suggested by me in a former part of this essay.

Comparative religion is another science which demands attention, when we wish to inquire into the origin of races, and it is undoubtedly of immense importance. Unfortunately the Bantu's religious ideas seem rather vague. We have already mentioned that Bishop Callaway's attempts to get at the core of the Zulu's idea of a God, met with but scant success, and attempts made by other missionaries among various Bantu tribes have not given much better results.

It has often been said that the Bantu have " Ancestor-worship," but I doubt whether this is correct in the main. That he worships the ancestors of his chiefs, or rather the " spirits " of departed chiefs, is undoubtedly true, but I question whether a Zulu or Kosa would worship the spirit of his great-grandfather. It is true that when a certain snake enters a hut, he is left in possession and not harmed in any manner, because it may contain the " spirit " of So-and-So, probably one who lived formerly on or near the spot where the hut stands. But, as I am not aware that the " spirits " are ever considered to be embodied in any other animal than snakes,* I am inclined to call this *Serpent-worship*. This certainly would agree with the Indian origin of the Bantu, a matter I shall refer to somewhat later.

The various Bantu names for " God " are very dangerous to use, except in certain clear instanecs. In some dictionaries the Bantu word for God looks suspiciously like a word coined for the purposes of religion and Bible-translation by the missionaries. Such is, for instance, the Luganda word *Katonda*, which means " the Creator," from the verb *tonda* = to make, to create." But some Bantu words for the idea *God* are certainly capable of explanation. The Secwana *Modimo*, for instance, reminds us strongly of the Assyriän *Dimmeru*, in Sumerian

---

*The case of the *Siboko*, or animal worshipped or " danced " to, so common among the Bechuana tribes, does not apply here, as this is evidently a relic of ancient *Tribal or family Totemism*, which has in reality nothing to do with religion.

An-ki-a, the God of Heaven and Earth. *Mulungu*, the Mang'--
anja expression, is most probably connected with the old Bantu
langa = high, with which the Zulu *ilanga* = sun, is also connected.
I at first, indeed, felt inclined to consider the word as a " per-
sonification " of the Sun, but came back from it, through the
fact that, as far as I am aware, there is no trace of Sun-worship
in any Bantu tribe, and the name for the Sun in most Bantu
tribes seems to be connected with an old Turanian root *ju* or
shu, meaning " warm." In Oruhima it is *izuba*, in Suaheli
jua, in Herero *e-yuva*, in Secwana *tsatsi*; in Mang'anja
dzuwa, in Luganda *juba*, etc.

Among all Bantu tribes we find a great respect for " spirits,"
which are generally inimical to mankind, and this form of be--
lief, with all its attendant institutions, such as medicine-men
and witch doctors, is still found in the Sakai of Malacca. It is
in reality the same as that *Shamanism* found all over Asia, in
places not touched by Brahmaism, Mahomedanism, or Chris-
tianity. It was the old *Bon* religion of Tibet, and it still plays
a not unimportant part in Northern Buddhism or Lamaism.*

Among a large number of Bantu tribes the " Spirits under
the Water," called in Zulu and Kafir the *Izizi*, play an important part. There can be no doubt but this is a very old Ugro-
Altaic belief. Among the ancient Sumerians the great God is
Hea, " the God of the Sea," who may, perhaps, be the same as
the much-revered *Ahti* of the Finns. Indeed, among the Finns
the water-deities and water-spirits play a very important part,
and their *Wesi-Husi*, by which they denote the " evil spirits of
the waters," are not only etymologically connected with the
Zulu *Izizi*, but bear also the same character. The Southern
Bantu's idea seems to be that these *Izizi* are really evil spirits,
and that is proved by the fact that sacrifices of an ox are made
to them, in cases of drowning, to induce them to release the
person taken by them. (See the well-known tale of the girl,
given by Dr. Theal in his " Kafir-Folklore.")

The Comparative Folklore of the Sakai, Semang, Indian
tribes and Bantu cannot be treated herein, as little as a comparison of the social customs. Each of these subjects contains
enough material to write a large-sized book on, and cannot be
discussed within the limits of this essay. But it is necessary
to mention here certain facts of historical nature.

In the first volume of his edition of Herodotus, p. 650, Raw--
linson states that in ancient times a Cushite or Ethiopian race
extended itself along the shores of the Southern Ocean from
Abyssinia to India. It started from the Indus along the sea-
coast through Beluchistan and Kerman, which latter (as Raw--
linson thinks) were the true countries of the Asiatic Ethiopians.

---

*The *Semang*, on the other hand, adore a Thunder-God (*Kari*), and of this
religion there seem to be considerable traces among the Hottentot as well as
among several Bantu tribes.

That the Asiatic Ethiopians of Herodotus did *not start* there, but in the Peninsula of Malacca, or in some country *south* of it, I have tried to show, and I have also attempted to show that the Semang and after them the Sakai moved to India. There is, as Caldwell has shown, proof that the present Dravidian races (which are nearest the Sakai and may have been caused by a fusion of Jakun and Sakai) lived in ancient times in Northern India, when Southern India was inhabited by what is called a Kolarian race, but which was probably a Semang race, and by an old diminutive race of which the Veddahs of Ceylon are the remains.

But Semang and Sakai mixed, and perhaps both even mixed with the Jakun, and a new race arose. What that race called itself we do not know, but when the Aryan entered India he called these people the *Nagas*, or the *Snakes*. How this name arose is very difficult to tell. It may be that this race had developed a *Serpent-worship*, the traces of which are still found among several aboriginal tribes of the Malayan Peninsula. It may be that these people called themselves with some word resembling *Naga*, and which the Aryans took over and made *Naga* of, because these people proved their worst enemies.*

The Tibetans called these people the *Klu* (pronounced *lu*), and this probably because the *Nagas*, with whom they were acquainted, were living along the shores of the Indus and its tributaries, for the *Klu* (as well as the *Naga*) were supposed to live in the rivers, and in Tibetan *klun* is a " river or stream."†

At the time of the invasion of India the *Nagas* seem to have principally lived along the Indus, and at the mouth of this river. The researches of Sir Thomas Holdrich and of Surgeon-Major C. F. Oldham (see his " The Sun and the Serpent," London, 1904) have shown that in very early times the race in the neighbourhood of the mouths of the Indus was not only highly civilised, but that it was a great sea-faring race, which founded several colonies on the West Coast of India, even as far as Malabar and Ceylon. Cunningham (quoted in Sir H. M. Elliot's " Races of the North-Western Provinces of India," vol. I., p. 113) connects these Nagas with the *Takkas* in the Punjaub, and thus places them between the Jhelum and the Indus, and Beames (who edited Elliot's work) places them even as far north as Kashmir.

---

*That seems to be the opinion of Lefmann in his " Geschichte des alten Indiens," page 366 (Berlin, 1890). In *Annamese* or *Mon*, which, as already said, is very nearly related to *Semang*, *ngu'o'i* is *man*, and the *Nagas* may have, as several nations have done, simply called themselves *men*. *Naga* in the meaning of " snake " is certainly not Aryan in origin, but is found in Siamese, and in certain non-Aryan languages in India. The true Aryan for snake is *Sarpa*.

†The name *klun* is still that of one of the non-Aryan tribes of India, and in Burmese, Sak and other languages, *lu* (which is the modern form of *klu*, and agrees with the pronunciation of the Tibetan word) means *man*. In Sumerian too *lu* means man, and the compound *a-za-lu-lu* is used in the sense of *mankind*.

F

There are certain expressions in Tibetan regarding these *Nagas* or *Lu*, which strongly seem to bear out Cunningham's and Beames' ideas. The Tibetans consider the *Lu* as a kind of demigods, having human heads and the body of a serpent.* They were believed to be the guardians of great treasures underground, a myth which clearly refers to their being merchants and traders, who brought treasures from the low country to the high plateau of Tibet. This is, in my opinion, clearly proved by an old Tibetan Festival, called the *Lu-theb*, which is defined as " the coming upwards of the *Lu* from their retreats in summer," while another expression *Lu-dog*, means " the retiring of the *Lu* to their abodes in the nether regions," and this was fixed at the beginning of winter. Now this clearly applies to the traders along the banks of the Indus, who each summer (the only time when the high mountain passes could be crossed) went to Ladakh and neighbouring countries with their wares, and returned home before the winter had covered the passes with snow.

The name or syllable *lu* appears in the designations of a large number of nations and places in Western Asia, and in my opinion this proves how far this race, *i.e.*, the Ugro-Altaic race, once spread. In the Bible we find the *Ludi* as the name for a race in Asia Minor, where we also have the Graecicized forms of *Lydia* and *Lykia*.†

We further have the district of *Luristan*, in Persia, which means really " the dwelling of the mountain *Lu*," *ri* being a common Turanian name for ' mountain.' "

This brings us to the word *Luganda* in Africa. *U-ganda* is the name of the country at present ; the people are called *Bagunda* (singular *Mogunda*), and the language is called *Luganda*. But the prefix *lu*, as the prefix for a language in Bantu, is absolutely unknown, and in accordance with Bantu etymology, the language should be called *Siganda* or *Seganda*. Under such circumstances I am convinced that we have to do here with a confusion of ideas and expressions, of which there are many other examples in the Bantu dialects. I am of opinion that the original name of the country was *Luganda*. If so, the etymology of the word is perfectly clear, viz., from *Lu* (the name of the old Nagas) and *gan*, the very common word in Turanian and Altaic for " garden," but also meaning

---

*Actual representations of such *Nagas* are found in Indian sculpture. Is it not possible that the *Nagas*, sailing as they did in boats and ships (which glided over the water as a serpent on the land) were therefore represented with bodies of a serpent ? In the Sumerian story of *Oannes*, who came to the mouths of the Tigris and Euphrates in a ship, we find the same connection of the *head* of a man and the *body* of a fish.

†Both *Lydia* and *Lykia* can easily be explained. *Lydia* was *Lu-de* = the Lu-community from Tibetan (Turanian) *de* = race, tribe, community. *Lykia* would be a compound of *Lu* and the Sumerian (*i.e.*, Ugro-Altaic) *ki* = land, and thus mean the " land of the *Lu*."

" land." In Sumerian *gan* is " a field," and *gana* is " a garden." The word is, on that account, also found in Semitic. Thus *Gan-Edin*, the garden of Paradise, really means " the Garden in the Plain," Assyrian *Gan-Edinnu* In the *Luganda* language we find the same root (with k =g) in *eki-kan-de*, which means " a deserted garden."

There is another word of importance in the Luganda language in connection with this matter, and that is *olulimi* =language. This is evidently a combination of *o* (the article) *lu* =people (the *Lu*) and *eme* =voice. (Compare Mongolian *ama*, and in other Altaic languages *imi* =voice.) The second *l* is merely euphonic, in accordance with a false concord.*

Now it is an undoubted fact that in Luganda we have a very old Bantu language, which has clearer affinities with the Manchu·branch of Ugro-Altaic than probably any other known Bantu dialect. It is also a fact, proved by the traditions of several Bantu tribes, that the regions near Lake Victoria Nyanza was the ancient and central home of the Bantu.

But how did the first Bantu get there ? This is a question which at present it is very difficult to answer, but after having taken all facts into consideration, I am inclined to think that the Bantu came to Africa *by sea* and not overland. The Hottentot may have come to Africa as a Semang overland, and he was probably followed by Sakai tribes who became the ancestors of the Gallas, Somali and other Hamitic tribes of North Africa. But the earliest Bantu must have come much later. At all events it certainly is remarkable that on the Egyptian monuments of early date we find no picture of a Bantu, nor do we find any description of Bantu tribes.†

In the second volume of his Herodotus, Rawlinson mentions an invasion into Africa of Asiatic Ethiopians about the year 1300 B.C. ·Unfortunately I have not been able to trace his authority, but upon the supposition that with Asiatic Ethiopia he means the country which the Greeks called *Gedrosia* and we *Beluchistan* (which is clearly the Eastern Æthiopia of Herodotus), I am inclined to believe that we have here a trace of the first Bantu invasion.

It is fairly certain that after the conquest of the northern part of India by the Aryans, that part of the population which we have denoted as *Klu* or *Nagas* was dispersed. A section of them sought refuge in the jungle regions, now known as *Nagpur*, a hilly and nearly inaccessible region, where even to-day we find a number of tribes which bear the name of *Nagas*,

*It is remarkable that the Luganda name for a " gardener " contains apparently the same root, as it also is *omu-limi*. But here the *limi* is quite another word, and is related to the Zulu *lima* = to cultivate, a word that is found in a number of Bantu dialects.

†Dr. G. M. Theal, however, has informed me that in the British Museum he has seen some relief work, which clearly represents Bantu men and women. As, however, he does not know from what period the representation dated, this leaves the matter as far as it was.

and whose languages bear marked relations to the Bantu dialects. Others sought refuge in the hills south of the Himalaya, from Nepaul to Assam. Again others, and probably those who were living in the Indus valley, crossed the mountains to the west and settled in Beluchistan, where a part of them continued their seafaring life, and another part became nomadic cattle-farmers. These were the ancestors of the present *Brahui*, whose name is probably derived from the old Turanian (Tibetan) *ba-hjo* =herdsman, with the often inserted *r*. In Tibetan *ba-glan-spyod* is the name of a country, west of India, so-called because cows feed on the land, and form the main wealth of the inhabitants. This I take to mean the northern portion òf Beluchistan.

The Brahui language is considered by competent authorities as belonging to the Dravidian language group, but it certainly has many Ugro-Altaic expressions in it. So has the *Baluchi* language, and so' has *Sindhi*, the language spoken along the lower course of the Indus. Sindhi has, like Baluchi, a strong Aryan element, and the former language is rightly considered as belonging to the Aryan group, though it certainly contains elements which are non-Aryan. In ancient times the number of these non-Aryan elements was undoubtedly larger than at present. Now it certainly is remarkable thàt several old Bantu words find their equivalents in these three languages, as the following examples will show :—

(1) Bantu *ngombe*, the general name for the ox, is a pure non-Aryan word, found in Khamti and Laos respectively as *ngo* and *ngoa*, and in Kuswar, Pakhya, Dadhi and Denwar as *gai*. In Sindhi it is *guan*.*

(2) Luganda (one of the oldest of the Bantu languages) has for " bullock " *endawo*. Oshikuanjama and Suaheli have for male animals *ndume*. In Sindhi we find the related *dana* = bullock.

(3) Mashona *gara* =to inhabit, clearly agrees with Sindhi *ghar* =a house, which is found in several of the non-Aryan languages of India. Dadhi and Denwar have *ghar* ; Kuswar has *ghara*.

(4) Mashona *bhati* =plank, which appears in Kongo as *ebaya* and *ebandu*, and in Luganda in *olu-bawo* is clearly the Sindhi *patt* =plank.

(5) The Zulu-Kafir *amasi* =sour milk is clearly the Baluchi *mass* =curd butter, or better, milk mixed with buttermilk.

(6) In Brahui the name for *Sorghum vulgare*, our " kafir-corn,' is *juar*, and this name is fairly common throughout India for the plant. Does not this agree with *juala*, the Zulu-Kahr name of the beer, made specially from kafir-corn ?

---

*Although at present found in India in several non-Aryan languages, it is not unlikely that the root *go* (*gom* or *gor*) has been loaned from the Aryans, who probably introduced the domesticated ox into India.

(7) Mashona *run-zhi* = a needle (where *run* is a prefix) is connected with Sindhi *sui* = a needle. In Permian *si* is " thread," and the Finnish *sui* has the same meaning. We have thus here the very same substitution which we find in some of the Bantu dialects. So Zulu has *usungulu* for needle, while Kafir has *usinga* for thread.

Many more examples might be given. So *Pushtu*, or the language of the Afghans, which contains many old Ugro-Altaic words among its mixed vocabulary, has *khaza* for woman, which agrees with the Bantu well-known *kazi*.

On these grounds I feel inclined to believe that the first invasion of Bantu in Africa came from some country near the mouth of the Indus, or a little to the west of it, and this would agree with the account given by Rawlinson. These probably landed in the present Somali-land (the ancient *Punt*) and driving the old Hottentot population before them, made their way to the neighbourhood of Lake Victoria Nyanza, where a portion of them settled, while another portion straightway worked their way to the west, where they became the ancestors of the Dualla, Mpongwe and other Bantu tribes of West Africa.

Naturally this is a *theory*, and such, I am afraid, it must always remain ; but at all events it is a theory with *some* evidence at the back of it, and as such it has a right to existence and to be carefully considered.

Of the *second* invasion of Bantu in South Africa we have, however, more historical and trustworthy data. I have already shown that on account of the ancient Babylonian and Sumerian elements in some of the Bantu dialects, this invasion must have come from the mouths of the Tigris and Euphrates.

At the mouths of these rivers many of the old Sumerians had taken refuge, and their number had undoubtedly been strengthened by many Semites, who for some reason or other had considered it advisable to leave their original habitations. Nominally subject, these " Men of the Sea Coasts " were in reality independent of Babylonia, though there never seemed to be any trouble between them and the authorities. Matters changed, however, when, about the year 900 B.C., Babylonia became a dependency of Assyria, and the so-called King of Babylonia was really an Assyrian vassal. Many Babylonians, dissatisfied with the new regime, must have gone to the Coast, and strengthened the independent community which gradually was formed there. This community at last became so strong, that it became an eminent source of danger to the Assyrian Empire, and it would seem that the Kings of Assyria began taking steps to stop the continual increase of power of the " Men of the Sea Coast." The latter, thereupon, rose in open rebellion about 720 B.C. and found a capable and daring leader in Merodach-Baladan, the same person mentioned in II. Kings, 20. For some time the rebels had it all their own way, because the attention of the Assyrian King was drawn to other, more important, matters. They conquered Babylon and seemed to have penetrated to the very borders of Assyria itself. Then, however, Assyria determined to subdue the foe. For a considerable time a keen struggle went on between Merodach-Baladan and his sons on the one side, and the Kings of Assyria on the other. But though the Men of the Sea Coasts were assisted by the Elamites and the tribes west of the mouth of the Tigris, the power of Assyria at length prevailed. The rebels were completely vanquished ; a huge slaughter took place, and those who did not fall by the sword left the country and sought refuge in the islands of the Persian Gulf. But Esarhaddon, the King of Assyria, equipped a large fleet and, attacking the rebels in the islands, succeeded in driving them even out of this refuge.

It is more than likely that the men who were thus driven out of their country, were aware that in or near Somaliland, on the neighbouring coast of Africa, there were living races who were nearly related to them. The Men of the Sea Coast were great mariners and traders, and if we remember that the great centre of trade in those days was the island of Socotra, it certainly is not surmising too much, if we believe that the Sumerians knew who lived in the country opposite Socotra. For that reason I believe that these fugitives, of whom nothing more is heard in Assyrian history, found a haven in Somaliland, and proceeded to join the Bantu tribes near the lakes. Assyrian chronicles place the flight of the Men of the Sea Coast in 680 B.C., so that this may also be considered the date when this *second Bantu invasion of Africa* took place.

It would seem that in the majority of cases the two elements coalesced, and this need not astonish us. The Sumerians originally came from the mouth of the Indus, as is clear from the Babylonian legend of the Deluge and the story of Gilgamesh, and hence there must have been a time when their forefathers and the forefathers of the first Bantu invaders were living together. The fact that there always has been, since the very earliest times of history, a considerable trade between the mouths of the Indus and the mouths of the Tigris and Euphrates, must have kept old tribal traditions alive, which would otherwise have sunk in oblivion.

It may be easily understood that the remnant of the Men of the Sea Coast which reached Africa, was but a poor remainder of the once powerful community. Their leaders, their priests, and their influential men had all fallen by the sword, and those who ultimately survived, must have belonged to what we might style " the lower classes of society." Hence the fact that nothing of the old Babylonian or Sumerian civilisation came over to Africa. Once in a strange country, shut out from their old home, the sea, the newcomers completely changed the tenor of their life, and became agriculturists and cattle-raisers, like the first Bantu had become. Gradually the distinction between the two elements wore away. But not altogether. The Babylonian element was strong and died hard, and the old Semitic linguistic factor was never altogether eliminated. It is impossible to-day, indeed, to draw a sharp line of demarcation between the various Bantu tribes, nor can we exactly tell which tribes came from the first invaders, and which tribes trace their origin to the later invasion. But, as a general rule, we may lay down that in those tribes, in whose language we find but single traces of Semitic (e.g., in Dualla, Mpongwe, Isubu, Luganda and Herero), we may see the descendants of the first Bantu invaders of Africa. But where, like in most of the Bakwena languages, and especially in the language of the Mashona, we find a very strong Semitic (not Arabian) element, we may fairly conclude that the origin of those tribes can be traced to the later invasion. But it should never be lost from view, that the Bantu has become a very mixed nation, and that at present we have but the *excrudescences* of the original elements, and not these elements themselves.

SECTION IX.

Those of my readers who are acquainted with the peculiarities of the Bantu languages may perhaps say that the foregoing paragraphs are all very nice and true, but that they do not throw any light upon two very important matters, namely, the *Prefixes of the Bantu languages* and the *Concord of the Bantu sentence.*

I readily admit that these questions are of the highest importance, and that, unless I can give a satisfactory solution of them, my foregoing theories will not carry much weight. For that reason I shall discuss these questions here, even at the risk of making this essay considerably longer than I originally intended.

I am quite aware that my solutions of these problems run completely counter to the at present generally accepted theories of Bantu philology, but that is not my fault. Bleek, Kolbe and, in fact, all other Bantu scholars seem to have considered that the *prefixes* were the peculiar and characteristic stamp of the Bantu languages, that they originated within Bantu itself, and that, indeed, Bantu had a philology peculiarly its own, widely differing from that of the other language groups. Hence they originated a system of *classifiers*, and to every singular *prefix* a plural *prefix* was assigned. At first sight it would seem that the spirit of the Bantu languages is really in accord with the principles thus laid down. So in Kafir the *m* or first-class nouns form their plural in *ba*, and the *m* or second-class nouns form their plural in *mi*. Various attempts have been made to show that words signifying a certain class of objects, are compelled by linguistic laws to have a special prefix, and Bleek as well as Kolbe have displayed a great deal of original acumen and ingenuity in attempting to show what the form of these classifying prefixes were. It is very doubtful in how far these attempts have been successful, and, personally, I feel compelled to state that these attempts have done more to complicate Bantu than anything else, while they have tended to place Bantu philology upon an absolutely false basis. For the idea up till now entertained that Bantu has a system of philology peculiarly its own, is beside the mark ; if it were it would, from a scientific point of view, imply that the Bantu race, as a collection of human beings, had an evolution of its own, independent from and unconnected with other human races. In other words, there must, then, once have existed a specific anthropoid ape, from which the Bantu race evolved. There is nothing which entitles us to such a supposition, and every bit of true Bantu philology pleads against that view, for all the general rules of philology, and all the principles of phonology, which apply to other Turanian languages are also applicable to the Bantu languages.*

The real facts are these :

The oldest languages of the world made use of a system of *prefixes*, *infixes* and *suffixes*. This has, in the case of the Mon-Khmer language (which is one of the parent languages of Bantu, and probably represents the Semang in its purest form), been shown by Schmidt, as quoted by Skeat and Blagden (in their aforementioned work, vol. II., p. 447). Thus in Khmer we have :

kat	= to cut
khnat	= measure
kunat	= piece
thkat	= pain
tamkat	= suffering
skat	= to cut off
sangkat	= division
pangkat	= to divide

where we find that by the addition of various *prefixes* and *infixes* different meanings are given to the root *kat*. .

---

*This naturally implies that I do not accept the so-called *pronominal* theory in Bantu. Indeed, I consider the idea that the *prefixes* were derived from the *pronouns*, to be historically impossible. Pronouns are late developments in the history of language, and are generally *shortened* forms of original personal *nouns*. That some original *prefixes* were afterwards used as *pronouns*, is an assertion I could agree to ; the reverse supposition I cannot subscribe to. *Prefixes* and *determinatives* belong to the oldest forms of languages.

In Semang and Sakai we find a similar system, though the matter does not seem to be thoroughly investigated. (See Skeat and Blagden, *op. cit.*, II., p. 774.) We have in Semang apparently a number of *prefixes*, such as *ke, pe, ta, ba,* etc., and in Sakai also a number such as *he, che, ke, te,* etc. In how far these are *classifiers* is a matter which has not yet been examined, but in *Annamese,* which is a pure *Mon* language, there exist a large number of classifiers, such as *banh* (for round things), *bo* (for things which form a " totality "), *cay* (for trees, plants, and things made of wood), *mieng* (for soft things), *so'i* (for ropes, threads, etc.), *dam* (for plantations and gardens), etc.

When the Semang and the Sakai went to India many of the dialects seem to have lost this peculiar power of formation, and to have adopted rather a system of *affixes.* Yet, some of these prefixes can be traced in a few languages, and especially in the *Naga* languages. So in *Angami Naga* we find *tefüh* = a dog ; where *te* is a prefix, which is dropped the moment the word is compounded with another, f.i. *fühpfö* = a male dog ; *fuhkru* = a bitch. In *mithu* = cow, *mi* is a prefix ; in *thenu* = goat, *the* is a prefix. In *Ao Naga, ta* is a common prefix in adjectives, and *ku* and *mang* are verbal prefixes, etc. Several instances could be drawn from other non-Aryan languages of India to show that this prefix and classifier-system formerly held sway in them, but has been lost. Thus :

Chepang *yuk* = " monkey " is Brahmu *pa-yuk.* So the root *pe* = to speak. is in Kami *ta-pe,* while " to be silent " is in Brahmu *ma-pe,* where *ma* is the prefixed negation. Khamti *wan* = sun becomes in Laos *kang-wan.* So the root *ni* = day or " sun " becomes in Bodo *di-ni,* in Kumi *ka-ni,* in Singpho *si-ni,* in Lepcha *sak-ni,* in Kami *ma-ni* ; the root *chu* = water is in Gyarung *ti-chi,* and so on.

In the Tibetan language we evidently had originally a complete system of *prefixes* or *classifiers,* which have now worn down to the so-called *prefix-letters* which, though written, are not pronounced any more, and have nearly all been lost in *Lepcha,* which is nearly related to Tibetan.

It would seem, thus, that in the Ugro-Altaic languages there arose a tendency to get rid of the *prefixes,* and to use *affixes* instead, and this naturally did away with the principle of classifiers. In Japanese we· find, however, a trace of the prefix-principle, in the fact that the plural of several words is still formed by prefixing some noun or expression of multitude, a system which is regularly followed still in Annamese, and of which examples will be given later.

It is a remarkable fact that some of the *prefixes* in Bantu are used in some of the other Ugro-Altaic languages as *affixes.* Thus the prefix *ku* (or *uku*) which in most Bantu languages is the prefix of the *infinitive* of the verb (or, to be more correct, the *noun-form* of the verb) is found in Mongolian and related languages, as an *affix* with the same meaning. In Mongolian it is known as the infinitive noun ending. So *ire-ku* is " the coming "; *ja-bu-chu* (chu = ku) is " the going." Turki has the same affix *ku* or *gu*, though in most cases the initial consonant is dropped. In Jakutish we have *kor* = to see, and *kor-u* (for original *kor-ku*) for " the seeing, sight."

So we have in several Bantu languages a *prefix lu*, which often forms nouns from verbal roots. In Mongolian the *affix l* has the same effect, and a strengthened form *lik* in Turki is the same.

It may seem to be rather peculiar to maintain that, within the limits of *one* group of language, there should be a change from *prefixes* to *affixes*. And yet the phenomenon is really a very common one among three very nearly related languages, of the Aryan group, viz., *German, Dutch and English*, languages so nearly related, that they might be called *Teutonic dialects*. Yet it is a very easy matter to show that, what are *prefixes* in Dutch and German, are *affixes* in English, and no less easy is it to show that the *prefixes* are older.

(*a*) In Dutch and German we have a prefix *be*, which has been nearly* completely lost in English, and the place of which in English is taken by a preposition *after* the verb, which from a true philological point of view is really an *affix*.

Dutch	*be*-loopen	is English	to walk *over*.
,,	*be*-leggen	,, ,,	to place *in*.
,,	*be*-vliegen	,, ,,	to fly *at*.
German	*be*-sprechen	,, ,,	to talk *over*. or *about*.
,,	*be*-dauern	,, ,,	to be sorry *about*.
,,	*be*-denken	,, ,,	to think *over*.

(*b*) German	*aus*-gehen	is English	to go *out*.
,,	*aus*-suchen	,, ,,	to seek *out*.
,,	*aus*-blasen	,, ,,	to blow *out*.
Dutch	*uit*-halen	,, ,,	to take *out*.
,,	*uit*-geven	,, ,,	to give *out*.

| (*c*) German | *auf*-stehen | is English | to stand *up*. |
| ,, | *nieder*-sitzen | ,, | to sit *down*. |

and many similar examples.

It is true that in the examples under (*b*) and (*c*) the prefixes in German and Dutch are separable, and can be put *behind* the verb in·certain flectional forms, but this really does not affect the question, and it certainly *cannot* be done with the examples

---

*I say *nearly* because we still find this *prefix* in the English words *bedaub, besmear, bespeak, beware,* etc. As the Dutch and German prefix *be* is rendered by various prepositions, so the prefix *be* in these English words has really different meanings.

under (a). The fact that in English the *prepositional affix* is written separately from the root-word, does not affect the question either, for this is a mere *spelling* and not a *structural* question. In speaking there is nothing to show that *talk-over* is structurally different from *be-sprechen*, except the fact that the one word has a *prefix* and the other an *affix*. In fact, in some words, such as the noun *lookout*, which is the Dutch *uitkijk*, the affix in English is actually written as *one* with the root, and there are several more expressions of a similar kind.

Everyone acquainted with the rudiments of Teutonic philology knows that the *prefix* construction is the older, and is · found in the immediate parent of German, Dutch and English, namely in Gothic, which is very rich in prefixes.

Of the Ugro-Altaic languages, outside of India, the oldest representative we are acquainted with, is undoubtedly *Sumerian*.

Now in Sumerian we have certainly prefixes, and probably, too, a system of *determinatives* or *classifiers*, which were taken over to a considerable extent by Assyrians.

As regards the prefixes, we have first the series *a, e, i, u. Prince*, in his Sumerian Dictionary, vol. I., p. xvii., says that these prefixes have an " abstract signification," a term which is somewhat difficult to understand. I am inclined to believe that in reality these prefixes were the demonstrative article *a* = this, used as the article *the* or *a*. We find the same phenomenon in *Lhota Naga*, where every word, if not otherwise defined, takes a prefix *o*. In Annamese we also find an article, and the fact that in Bantu we have this same prefix *a, e, i, u*, with evidently the force of the article, makes me think that the Sumerian prefix had the same effect.

> *ki* as prefix in Sumerian denotes place ;   ·
> *lu* denotes the *agent*
> *sa* denoted, as Prince maintains, abstract relationship.
> *nam* (=face) is an abstract element, usually denoting a state or condition.

Of the *determinatives* in Sumerian we really know very little, except their Assyrian meanings. Before male proper names a sign was put, which is read as *dis* or *gis* in Sumerian ; before the names of tribes and professions, a sign which reads *amelu* = man in Assyrian, and which in Sumerian would read in full *mu-lu*, but as *determinative* probably read short, as *mul* or *mu*. Before trees and wooden objects a determinative was placed which in Sumerian was generally read as *is*, but sometimes as *mu* ; its Babylonian form was *isi*.

In discussing the Bantu prefixes and their origin, I shall have to refer often to these Sumerian prefixes and determinatives, which are undoubtedly closely connected with the old Bantu prefixes. In doing so I shall follow, for convenience sake, the generally accepted system of Bleek, as explained in his *Zulu-prefixes*, on page 161 of his " Comparative Grammar of South African languages." These are as follows, (*without the article*) !—

Singular.	Plural.
1. mu.	2. ba.
3. mu.	4. mi.
5. li.	6. ama.
7. isi.	8. izi.
9. in.	10. izin.
11. lu.	12. izi ; izin.
*	
14. bu.	
15. ku.	

There is only this difference between my arrangement and that of Bleek, that the latter considers the *a* of the 6th prefix and the *i* of the 8th, 9th, 10th and 12th prefixes as the article. I shall explain, somewhat later, why I differ from him in this view.

I. The 1st prefix *mu*.

It is generally considered by all Bantu scholars that this is the special prefix used to denote persons, and there can be no doubt that this is correct. It is undoubtedly the Sumerian determinative which was rendered in Assyrian as *amelu*. *Mu* is a very old name for *man*, or *human being*, and appears as *ma, me, mi, mo,* and *mu* in a large variety of languages.†

The root form of this word is found in the pure Bantu form *mu-tu*, met with in Aduma, a language which displays some remarkably pure forms ; the form is also found in Kinika. *Mutu* or any of its other forms is always used in Bantu to denote a *man, i.e.* a *male*, though in the plural it also includes *women*, and has then the general sense of *people*, a development which is evidently of late date. The root *ma* as meaning " human being " is already found in Sakai, and in Semang (with a prefix *ha*) as *ha-me*, and (with an affix) as *me-nik*.

In the Indian languages the word does not appear in its pure Bantu form,‡ but in Assyrian we have *mutu* in the sense of " husband," and in Tibetan we find a related form *mthu* in the meaning of " virile power." There can, however, be no doubt of the origin of the word. In Semang *tau* (*tu* in some

---

*The 13th prefix of Bleek is the diminutive *ka*, which is really an *infix*, and which I cannot consider here.

†See for particulars of this B. H. Hodgson's " Miscellaneous essays relating to Indian subjects " (Trübner's Oriental Essays), Vol. II., pp. 59-61;

‡In one Indian language *Mru*, man is *mru*, and this agrees with the Shuna *mrum* = man, and the Kikuya *murumo*. The Indian *Mru* probably stands for an original *mtu*, as the change from *t* to *r* is by no means uncommon in either the Indian languages or the Bantu dialects.

dialects) means " male," and with the prefix *mu* = human being, *mutu* would thus mean a " male human being," which is exactly its real meaning in Bantu.

In several Bantu dialects the word has, however, undergone remarkable changes. In Zulu it is *u-mu-ntu*, as usually written. This spelling is, however, really wrong, and should be *u-mun-tu*. The *u* is the article, *mun* is the nunated form of *mu*, that is, a form with an infixed *n*, which is a very common phenomenon in Bantu ; *tu* has remained unchanged. In Kafir the word is *umntu*, with elision of the vowel. In the Herero we have *o-mun-du*, perhaps formed under Sumerian influence, where *du* is " son " or " male," as well as *tur*, which latter is simply a strengthened form of *tu*. Secwana *mo-thu*, and Serotse *mo-nu* are deviations, the latter being perhaps connected with the very common non-Aryan Indian form *mana*. In Mang'anja we find the form *mu-ntu*, as Scott writes it. Scott wants to make out that this word consists of the prefix *mu* and *ntu* = matter, thing, and that the word would thus really mean the " man-thing." I am afraid this view is indefensible. The plural of the Mang'anja word is *Antu* (for *Bantu* or *Wantu*) and this would not agree with Scott's idea, but shows that Mang'-anja evidently has worn-down forms, and as such I can only consider the Mang'anja form the same as Zulu *u-mun-tu*, with *nunation*, but elision of the article.*

Upon the principle of this rootform *mu-tu* is probably based the first prefix, which is used for personal designations. In many dialects its combination with the article *u* (or its variations), namely, *umu*, is shortened into *um*, especially in Zulu.

II. The *second* prefix of Bleek is the prefix *ba*, which is used to form the plural of the words of the first class.

There has been a good deal of unnecessary speculation about the origin of this and the other plural prefixes in Bantu, due to the fact that the philological position of the Bantu languages was not understood, and that a special system of philology was thus built up by the first Bantu scholars, such as for instances the Pronominal System of Kolbe in his " Language study based upon Bantu " (London, 1888), a work upon which evidently a good deal of time and great ingenuity has been spent, but which is really useless.

In all the old *Mon-Khmer* languages the plurals were formed in two manners : (*a*) by repetition of the word, a form still found in Sumerian, and not infrequently met with even in Bantu ; (*b*) by prefixing to the singular some word or syllable

---

*I admit that there is some difficulty about the Mang'anja form, in view of Manganja *chi-ntu* = a thing, *i.e.* any thing without life. There certainly is an old Bantu word *ntu* = " anything that has a shape, or is perceptible by the eye," and a very clear Turanian origin can be found for this word. But the composition of *chi-ntu* is not yet quite clear to me, and I am not prepared at present to agree with Scott that *mu-ntu* expresses " a living thing " and *chi-ntu* " a dead thing." •

implying multiplicity. Thus in Annamese the idea *men* can still be expressed in these two forms : ngu'o'i ngu'o'i = men (by repetition of the singular ngu'o'i) or by *nhung ngu'o'i*, really meaning *all* men. In *Semang* and *Sakai* the same systems are followed. In several of the Indian languages of this group, we find the same, with this difference, that here has already taken place the change from *prefixes* to *affixes*. Thus in L*hota Naga* the nouns of multitude (*oten, oyo, elam*, etc.) are put *behind the nouns*, which they qualify. In *Ao Naga* " prungla " is used in the same manner to form plurals.

Now, in Annamese we find the prefix *bo* used to express a *totality*, *i.e.* a composite body of homogeneous parts, *e.g.* a crowd of men. In Japanese this word in the form of *ban*, meaning at present " ten thousand," but formerly " any large number," is still used as a *plural prefix* to many words, especially such as have been introduced from the Chinese language. Thus *nin* (originally Chinese) means *man*, *ban-nin* = people, the men. *Mots* is thing, *bam-mots* = things.* This plural prefix *ba* or *ban* is clearly found in the language of Malacca, where we have in Semang *ba-lo* = many, in Sakai *bi*-ga = many, and *e-bah* = all ; in Jakun we find *ban-yak* = many.

The root of this plural prefix is evidently the old verb *ba* = to divide, found in Sumerian as well as in Bantu (Zulu *aba*, Luganda *ga-ba*). The most ancient form of the verb was *ka* (compare the above cited Mon-Khmer *kat* = to cut), and it still has that old form in Semang, and in several Bantu languages (Kongo *kaya*, Bobangi *kakola*, Zulu (si)-*ka* = to cut, etc.), but as already shown, there was always a tendency in several Ugro-Altaic languages to change *k* into *b* or *p*.†

This *ba* or *ban* appears in a number of Bantu words, all expressing multitude. A few may be quoted here :

Secwana	bantsi	= many.
,,	banwe	= some.
Bobangi	bala	= to count.
Zulu	isibalo	= a number.
,,	balela	= to numerate.
Luganda	ba-la	= to produce.
Dualla	ben-ga	= to increase.
,,	a-ba	= to divide.

Now, it is this *ba*, this usual sound expressing " division " or " plurality " which underlies the Bantu prefix of the plural *ba*.

For instance, the singular of the ancient word for man was *mutu*, and the plural " men," was formed by the prefix *ba*, so

---

*The fact that the *n* of the original *ban* changes in the latter case to *m* (by assimilation) is strong evidence in favour of the supposition that the *n* of *ban* is merely a case of *nunation*, and that the original word was really *ba*, which agrees with Annamese *bo* and Sumerian *ba*.

†The *p* form is still found in Finnish *paljon* = many, which is exactly the form of Semang *balo*, with a slight phonological change.

that we first had *ba-mu-tu*. But the *m* had after the labial *b* a natural tendency to change to *n*, especially in quick pronunciation, or to express the process more clearly, the second vowel *u* probably fell out first (a very common thing, *é.g.* in the Indian languages) and we had thus *bamtu*. But *m* will, before *t*, always assimilate to the hard *n*, and thus we get *Bantu* or, with the article, *a-bantu*.

When once *mu* had become the singular prefix to certain words upon the *mu-tu* idea, it was but natural that, upon the same analogy the *ba* prefix of *ba-ntu* should be used to express the plural form of this class of words.*

What strengthens my explanation, as given above, is the fact that in Assyrian, which, as we know, took over several expressions from Sumerian, we find the word *banutu* in the expression *mar-banuti* (plural, or perhaps genitive), which is generally translated as " the sons of the free," or the " sons of the noblemen," but which, considering its ideograph *Tur-Kak*, I should feel inclined to consider as meaning the " men of the people," *i.e.* the lower free classes,† in opposition to the official and priestly classes, a designation found exactly in the same manner in English history, and in fact in the history of all European States during the early middle ages, and which even in Rome we find in *homo liber* as opposed to the *liberti* and the *servi*. In this expression I certainly consider the *ba* a plural prefix, and I may in support thereof point to the Assyrian *ba-chulati* = soldiers. If this surmise is correct we have the remarkable fact that Bleek in giving the name of *Bantu* to what had been before called " the Kafir races of Africa," has unconsciously revived one of the actual old names of the race. If not, then such a coincidence of nomenclature is " beyond the ken of science. "

III. and IV. The consideration of Bleek's third and fourth prefixes, viz., singular *ma*, plural *mi* cannot conveniently be treated here, but must stand over until we have treated the other prefixes.

V., VI. and XI. I shall now first discuss Bleek's fifth prefix *li*, as found in Zulu, and in order not to have unnecessary repetition, I shall include in this discussion the eleventh prefix, which in Zulu is *lu*.

---

*This naturally implies that the *present* system of *prefixes* or *classifiers* was developed in Bantu itself, after it parted from the parent languages. This I certainly would not deny, but my contention is that the *principle* underlying these prefixes or classifiers, and the *original* forms of these classifiers must be deduced from the more *ancient* languages. The mistake, thus far made, has been to consider the *principle* as well as the *form* as of pure Bantu origin.

†The expression is taken from the *Behistun* inscription of King Darius, and at such a late period there had taken place no doubt considerable changes in the original meanings of expressions, and in Darius' time *mar-banuti* may have been " the sons of the noblemen," or " patricians. "

I strongly doubt whether, originally, this *li* and *lu* were really prefixes. In several Bantu languages they do not exist at all. According to Bleek they are in Kikambo *i*(y) or *u*, which is equivalent to saying that they do not exist, for the *i* or *u* here is the mere old Bantu article. In *Shambala* the fifth prefix has disappeared altogether, for if Bleek and Seidel maintain that the fifth prefix is Shambala in *n* or *m*, they are completely wrong, for the *n* and *m* here simply represent *nasalisation*, and this is clear from the very fact that this class has in Shambala no actual plural, but the plural is the same as the singular.* In Herero the fifth prefix is lost, for the *e* for that class is simply the article *o* in a weakened form, and *Brinker* has correctly noticed this in his " Lehrbuch der Oshikuanjama " (Berlin, 1891, page 88, II part), though he is wrong in supposing that the old form was *eli*. But Herero has for the eleventh prefix *ru* (for *lu*), and Oshindonga and Oshi-kuanjama have *lu*, and the same is the case in Nano and Kongo ; Mpongwe has no prefix *lu*. Dualla has for the fifth prefix a very unusual and probably old Turanian syllable *di*, *dj* or *d*, which cannot be treated here, while Isubu has the same. It may thus fairly be concluded, that as this *lu* is not a *general* Bantu prefix, like most of the other prefixes, it has a foreign origin, and that I indeed believe to be the case.

There does, however, exist in some Ugro-Altaic languages an affix *l*, which may be the remains of an original fuller form, represented in Turki as *lik*. In Mongolian this affix *l* has, for all practical purposes, the force of an article. Thus *nom-la* = to learn, while *nom-lal* is the *learning ; mede* is " to know," and *medel* is " the knowing " or " knowledge," and it would thus seem that this *l* forms nouns from verbal roots, and in *Jakutish* the *l* does the same.

In Arabic and in several of the so-called Hamitic languages in the North-East of Africa, which have taken over several elements of the old South Arabian languages (Himyaritic, Minaean, and Sabaean) we find an article composed of a vowel and an affixed and sometimes prefixed *l*. In Classical Arabic we have *el ;* in Masai we have *ol* (masculine plural, *il*),and in *Bari* we find *lo* (probably due to metathesis).†

There can be little doubt, but at a very early period the Bantu invaders of Africa came into contact with these Hamitic races, which inhabited in those times not only Abyssinia and the present Somali and Galla-land, but also the regions of the Nile, north of Lake Albert Nyanza, and who may have penetrated even as far as the present British East Africa. At a later stage the Bantu certainly came in close touch with the

---

*This is accounted for partly by the fact that Shambala is one of those Bantu languages which has lost the ordinary *vowel-article*.

†I have not been able, thus far, to trace the origin of these forms.

Masai, which have always been a warlike race. If we compare, *e.g.*, the weapons of the Zulu tribes as well as some of their customs, with those of the Masai, one must come to the conclusion, that not only were some of the Bantu tribes in very close touch with this race, but that they·may even have been subjected by it.*

The Ugro-Altaic Bantu had its definite article, which was originally *a*, but which, in accordance with the ancient vocalic harmony (of which we still find part preserved in Bobangi); could become *e, i, o* or *u*. When the Bantu came into close contact with the Nilotic, Hamitic and Masai tribes their language was, to some extent, affected, and this would be especially the case with such Bantu tribes as were, for a longer or shorter time, subjected by those races. So it happened that in some of the Bantu languages the original article underwent a change, and added to its vowel the *lo* or *lu* of the Hamitic languages, and thus we have the *ilu* and *ulu* of Zulu-Kafir, and the *oru* (r = l) and *olu* of Herero, Oshindonga and Oshikuanjama. But these latter languages retained the fifth prefix as its original article, as did Nana and Kongo. The Mpongwe, a Bantu tribe, which evidently migrated to the west at a very early period, never came sufficiently under Hamitic influence to suffer any change in its article, and hence it kept its pure *i* and *o*.

It is remarkable that, though in *Luganda* we have the fifth prefix as *e*, 'this *e* is a so-called *explosive* one, which tends to show that a letter, probably *l* has fallen out. So *e'bere* (as written in Luganda) may stand for an older *el-bere*, and this is the more likely because the *pronominal* concord of this class is *li*. In Bobangi, again, *li* is only the *pronominal* concord in the plural, while *e* is the concord in the singular.

There are several linguistic phenomena in connection with these prefixes, which tend to show the correctness of this view. So we have in Bantu a root *zwe* or *zwi*, which originally meant " voice," and afterwards " country," a root, which is of undeniable Ugro-Altaic origin. In Zulu *zwi*, meaning ." voice," has the prefix *i*, while *zwe*, denoting " country," has the prefix *ili*. This certainly proves that the prefix *ili* cannot be a *classifier*, as has been maintained by several authors.

Another reason in favour of my theory is, that the plural of the fifth prefix is generally *ama*, that is, that it takes one of the *general plural* forms, and this is the same with the eleventh prefix, which usually has as plural the *general plural* form *izin*, *zim* or *izi*, which is also the plural of the ninth class.

---

*The Masai, I venture to suggest, are· probably the descendants of those *Asmach* mentioned in Herodotus II., 30, as being Egyptian soldiers who deserted and emigrated to Ethiopia. Herodotus places this emigration in the time of King Psammetichus, but it probably 'took place much earlier. In ancient Egyptian *Masu* actually means a " soldier," and in the Masai language there are several words of undeniable Egyptian origin, *e.g. keper* = above, *dito* = girl and others.

VII. and VIII. I shall now first discuss the seventh prefix of Bleek, *isi*, which forms its plural in the eighth prefix *izi*.

Bleek considers the *i* here as the article, but I think he is wrong here. We have here, as I shall show, an absolutely pure *classifier*, and the *i* of the article is probably contracted with the classifier *isi*, hence we have really *īsi*.

There can scarcely be any doubt but that this is a very old Ugro-Altaic prefix and classifier. In Sumerian we have the prefix *is* (*ish*) for all objects connected with trees or plants, or for anything made of wood or fibre; in general we may call it the *prefix of the vegetable world*. *Issu* in Babylonian means *plant, tree,* and its usual ideograph is a sign, which is usually read *is,* but seems to be read occasionally *mu.* Of the origin of this word there can be no doubt, as we find already in *Sakai isi* in the meaning of " wood," a root again met in the non-Aryan languages of India, as in Dhimal *sing,* Pahdi *si-ma,* Nachhereng *sa'a,* Angami Naga *si,* Sibsagor Miri *ising,* etc., all meaning " tree."*

In Sumerian we find this prefix in a large number of words, directly or indirectly connected with the vegetable kingdom, such as :

is-gusur	=	a beam.
is-na	=	a bed (made of wood).
is-su-dis	=	doorbolt (made of wood).
is-pan	=	bow.
is-ma-nu	=	cage.
is-gu-za	=	chair.
is-mar	=	chariot.
is-ter	=	forest, a tree.
is-sa-tur	=	a net (made of fibre).
is-sar	=	an orchard.
is-ir	=	a rope (made of fibre).

and a large number more.

In the Zulu and Kafir language we have, in a similar manner, a large number of words, connected with the vegetable world, which also have the prefix *isi*. Thus :

isi-biba	= (a herbal) antidote for snake-bites.
izi-kali (pl.)	= weapons (originally of wood, just like the Sumerian *is-ku* weapons, with which, indeed, the Zulu word is closely connected).
isi-dabene	= wild banana.
isi-tya	= basin (of wood).
isi-kapa	= blade of grass.
isi-nkwa	= bread.
isi-dhliso	= poison (vegetable).

*Under such circumstances it is very likely that the Bantu prefix is not derived from *Assyrian* or *Sumerian,* but directly from the parent-language.

isi-gabe	= young pumkin.
isi-konkane	= wooden pin.
isi-blenga	= raft.
isi-rongo	= screen (of mats).
. isi-tuniz	= shade (of bushes).
isi-bonda	= stake.
isi-guba	= hollow vessel (made from a gourd).
isi-nga	˙ = a clump of thorn-trees.
isi-pato	= handle (of wood).
isi-lando	= a needle (of thorn).*

and a host of others.

But *is* in Sumerian also meant *earth*, and it seems than the two words *is* were confused at an early period, a confusion which became strongly developed in Bantu. Hence *is*, even in Sumerian, is occasionally used as a prefix to things connected with the earth, *e.g. is-hu* = worm (really " earth-vermin "), *is-du* = to pull down (= to throw on the earth). In Bantu there are a large amount of such examples, *e.g.* in Zulu :

isi-bomvu	= red earth.
isi-buda	= red ochre.
isi-sindi	= sod.
isi-gagadu	= hard soil.
isi-daka	= black soil.
isi-sekelo	= foundation.
isi-za	= a plot of ground.
isi-kala	= a chasm.
isi-dindi	˙ = a clod of earth (really a bye-form of *isi-sindi*).
isi-wa	= a crag.
isi-makade	= a fixture.
isi-duma	= a mound.
isi-hambi	= a traveller (literally " one who goes over the ground ").

etc., etc.

It should be remembered that very often new words and ideas are formed from old ones, which latter were originally connected with plants or the ground, though the new ideas have no such affinity. In such cases, the new words would retain the prefix *isi*, in accordance with the old association of ideas. Thus in Sumerian *is-mi* means " protection," which has apparently nothing to do with plants or the ground. But the word originally meant " shade " or, literally, " the dark of the tree," and as " shade " was a " protection against the hot rays of the sun," it actually, by analogy, obtained that

---

*It is, however, more than likely that this is not really an *isi* prefix, but that the syllable *si* belongs to the root, and that the word is really *i-silando*.

meaning.* So the Sumerian *is-hu* = a bridegroom, has in itself nothing in common with a tree or plant, but originally the
word meant " the preparer of the hut," and the hut being
made of vegetable material, the word obtained the prefix *is.*.

Not unlikely the same psychological process took place in
Bantu, where we find numerous words, beginning with *isi*,
which do not at present have any apparent connection with
either the earth or the vegetable kingdom. In many cases in
Zulu and Kafir *isi* stands as an *apparent* prefix for words taken
over from English and Dutch beginning with *sh* or *sch*. The
sound *sk* the Bantu cannot pronounce, so he inserts the vowel
i between the *s* and the *k*, and as the words obtain the article
i, there originates an apparent prefix *isi*. In Bantu grammars
and dictionaries these words are really wrongly placed with
the prefix *isi*, though it would seem that the instinct of the
language considers them to belong to that class, on account
of the mere sound. So we have the Dutch *schaap* becoming
isikapu, *schip* = *isikepe*, *zens* = *isizenze* (this may be a *pure*
prefix), *sikkel* = *isikeli*, and several others might be mentioned.

In some cases the article *i* has *nunation* (adding of *n*). Thus
the Zulu *insikane* = " sedge, reed," ought to be *isi-kane* from
Assyrian *kanu* = reed or sedge. Zulu *insimu* (which in Kafir
has still been further deteriorated into *intsimi*) = field, is really
isi-mu, meaning " a land covered with vegetation," from *isi*
and *ma* = land. The nature of this *nunation* being misunder-
stood, these words are now considered as belonging to the
ninth prefix class.

The eighth prefix *izi*, *izin*, *izim*, I believe to have been simply
caused by the usual re-duplication for *plural* forms, so that we
had the series *isisi* = *issi* = *izi*. I am strengthened in this view
by the fact that in the *Shuna* language, we actually find the
form *zhinzhi* in the meaning of *many*. Once being adopted as
the plural of an important class of nouns, this form gradually
grew into what may be called a *general* plural form, and hence
we find it as plural prefix for the tenth and twelfth classes, a
clear proof of the fact that the Bantu have long forgotten what
was the original meaning of these *prefixes*.

VI. Now let us consider Bleek's *sixth* prefix *ama* which forms
the plural of the fifth class, and also, in some cases the plural
of some words of the *first* class, and is especially used in form-
ing the names of *tribes* or *nations*, such as, e.g., the *Amazulu*,
the *Amakosa*, *Amaswazi*, etc.†

I consider that the first origin of this plural prefix is in its
use as a tribal designation, and that originally, indeed, the

---

*We, in English, often use the word *shade* in the meaning of " protection,"
and even the word *umbrella*, through the same association of ideas.

†This tribal prefix *Ama* is only used in some Bantu languages ; a very large
number (*e.g.*, the Bechuana tribes) use *Ba* as the plural tribal prefix, and this
Ba is the same as the *second* prefix found in *Bantu*.

prefix meant " people, nation." There is to be traced a whole series of this word or expression *ama*, in the meaning of " people." In Semang we find for people *hame*, in Sakai *mai* and *mah*, in Lhota Naga we have *yam* (where the *y* is inserted) ; in Mandchu we have *amaga* = descendants, posterity ; in Turkish we have *amme* = people, and in Sumerian *amar* = posterity. In Tibetan and Lepcha, in which very few words begin with a *vowel*, we have the related forms *mi* = mankind,. and *mino* = nation, words found in several Indian non-Aryan languages. That in ancient West Asia the term was known as " nation," is clear from such names as the *Amorites* (= the people of the mountain), the *Amazones* (which has nothing to do with Greek *Zone*. but simply means the " fighting people ") and others, and it is probably a prefix in the Assyrian *amelu*, which must originally have been a plural form, meaning " mankind."*

For that reason I believe that *ama* was first used as a prefix to nations, as it still is in Sakai, and that hence we find its oldest form in *Amazulu*, *Ama* Xosa, etc., which really mean the " people of Zulu," " the people of Xosa," etc.

When once this *ama* was used for " people " or " nation,'" *i.e.*, a collection of men, it was used in " analogous cases, and so we find *ama-doda* = men (pl. of indoda) ; *ama-pakati* = the councillors ; *ama-hlwenpu* (Kafir) = poor men ; *ama-kwenkwe* = boys. Gradually its range stretched, and it was used even for collections of women, *e.g. ama-nkazana* (Kafir) = women ; *ama-kosi-kazi* (Kafir) = chiefs' wives.† At last, as in the case of *izi*, the prefix *ama* became a *general* prefix for the plural.. This must have taken place already at a time when the Bantu had not yet departed from their original Ugro-Altaic stem, for in Japanese we find *amata* in the meaning of " many," and in Sumerian *ama* has the meaning of " multitude."

I have already mentioned the fact that one has to be careful to distinguish *real* prefixes from *apparent* prefixes in Bantu, and it may be useful to illustrate this in connection with *ama*. It is generally considered by Bantu scholars, and practically by the Bantu themselves (because they use *plural* concords in connection with the words) that *amanzi*, meaning " water," *amasi* = fermented milk, and *amafuta* = fat, are real plurals. Yet this is absolutely wrong, and the words which are to-day *plurals*, were original *singulars*, and have only come to be considered plurals through false analogy.

---

*In how far this *ama* is connected with *ama* = mother. I cannot here discuss,. but I consider it quite likely that the latter is really the rootword.

†In the very remarkable Kafir *ama-nyange* = the people of old, *ama* has its. full force of " people." The etymology of *nyange* is doubtful ; it may mean the same as *Mang'anja* = the people of the waters ; but it might be that *nyange* actually stands for *Naga*, and that we have thus here one of the old: names for the Bantu.

I have already shown that in *amasi*, the *ma* belongs to the root of the word, which is clearly from the Beluchi *mass*=sour milk.

As regards *water*, there are two old roots to represent this element. The one is *mi*, *mu* or *ma* found already in Semang and Sakai, and changed into some Turanian dialects into *wa* (m=w), which originally meant the "water from heaven," namely *rain*. The other is *ti*, changed into most Turanian dialects into *si*, *chi* or *chu*, which meant the "water of rivers," *i.e.* the water on earth. In Sumerian we find the root *a*=water (which is probably=wa), and another related form *mu*, and we also find the form *a-me*, which is generally supposed to be a plural form, but which is possibly a conjunction of two synonomous roots.* Such conjunctions of synonomous roots are not uncommon in ancient Eastern languages, and *Hodgson*, *op. cit.*, vol. II., p. 69, gives the Ugrian *we-zi*=water, as example. Now Finnish has *wesi*, Hungarian has *viz*, and Japanese has *mu-zi*. Bantu *man-zi* is formed upon exactly the same principle. The *n* here is the ordinary *nunation*, as is clear from the Makua *mazi*, Sesuto *metsi* (where *ts*=z), and Jao *me-si*, while Kinika has *mazi*. The usual article *a* was placed in Zulu and Kafir before it, and so we have *amanzi*. In course of time *ama* was wrongly taken for the plural prefix, and hence Bantu scholars have been giving some of the most absurd etymologies for the word.

Amafuta is in exactly the same position, and is also a compound of *two* roots, meaning the same thing. In Sakai *mu*= fat ; in Sakai pä-o=fat. In several non-Aryan languages *mo-to* (where *to* is an adjectival affix)=fat, but in the same group *pi* and *phum* is also *fat*. In Khyeng *ma* is fat ; in Shan it is *phyee*. In Finnish we have *woi* (for *moi*)=butter ; in Magyar *vaj*=butter.

It is, therefore, clear that *ma-futa* (the ending *ta* is found in some of the Naga languages, *e.g.* in *peleta*=fat) is a compound of the two root-words. In Aduma fat =*evongo*, where we have only *one* root, agreeing with Magyar *vaj*.

XV. The fifteenth prefix of Bleek *ku* (with the article *uku*) is a purely Ugro-Altaic prefix. It is well known that in Bantu it forms *infinitives* and *gerunds*. That is exactly what the Mongolian affix *ku* or χu does, for which reason it is known in that language as the "Infinitive form." In Turki and in Jakutish we have several forms. In Manchu *ku* as affix denotes only "nomina actionis."

It is, in my opinion, most likely that all these endings are really different forms of an original *uku*="to make, to do," which is found in Sumerian as *aka* or *ag* (variant *kak*), in

---

Prince in his Sumerian lexicon ascribes the reading *mu* to Semitic influence, but this is clearly wrong. I must confess that Prince's work is really a very disappointing book, and is based upon completely wrong principles.

Baluchi as *kan-aga*, in Brahui as *kar*. In Baluchi *aga* is the ending of all verbs and expresses the *action*. In Semang *kai* = to make ; and in Sakai *ka* is actually found as a *verbal infinitive prefix*, *e.g. kabeh* = to build (root *beh* ; compare Annamese *bŭa* = to make) ; *kabuk* = to bind (root *buk*) ; *kātut* = burn (root *tut*) ; *katŭ* = to pour (root *tŭ*) ; *kajōn* = to give (root *jnō*), and a large number more, which the reader can easily find in the Vocabulary at the end of Skeat and Blagden's aforequoted work. It may be stated that in Sumerian this prefix does not seem to be found, but that it is still found as an *affix* in some words. Thut *ka-aga* = " to eat," is really " to work with the mouth," from *ka* = mouth, and *aga* = to work ; *mi-ga* = " to set (of the Sun)," is really " to make dark," from *mi* = dark and *aga* = to make.

In Kafir *uku* is the regular prefix for the infinitive ; in Zulu, and in nearly all Bantu languages it has the same force. In Zulu (like in Manchu) it is often used to form verbal substan-. tives ; thus *uku-mela* = opposition, from the verb *mela* = to oppose. In Kafir this is not so common, though we do find examples, such as *uku-fa* = death, from *fa* = to die.

Under such circumstances it is but natural that there is no plural form for this prefix.

XIV. The fourteenth *prefix* of Bleek is *bu*, with the article *ubu*.

I must confess that this prefix is connected with greater difficulties than any other, and that principally because throughout the Bantu languages this prefix, as a rule, is used to form so-called " abstract nouns."

In Turki and Mongolian we have an affix *bur*, which forms nouns for verbal stems, and most-of these nouns seem to be abstract. Thus, in Jakutish we have from the verb *tolno* = to pay, the noun *tolo-bur* = payment, while in Mongolian we have from the root *tail* = to declare, *tail-bur* = declaration. In the Turki languages *bar* means " existence " and " to exist." In Japanese *ba* = a state, condition. In Sumerian we have *bar* = body, form.*

The conception of " abstract ideas " must have been a fairly late idea in the development of the human mind. In the Naga languages very few abstract ideas are found, a fact remarked upon by Mrs. E. W. Clark in her " Ao Naga Grammar," p. 5. Sumerian too, possesses few abstracts nouns, and such as there are seem to be preceded by the prefix *nam* = fate, position. So, *nam-lu-gal-la* is used in the meaning of " Majesty," but literally it means " the position of a king." There is thus some reason for supposing that in Sumerian these abstract concep-

---

*This root is most likely connected with Sakai *ba-lo* = face, and *bāku* = to observe. The Semang form is *muku*, and this root is found in Sumerian and other Altaic languages as a parallel form. In Japanese *mukai* = to face ; in Sumerian *ma-char* is " front, appearance."

tions arose only after the Sumerian had been conquered by the Semites, whose power of abstraction was far larger. Now it would seem that this prefix *bu*, as "a sign of abstraction" is not present in some of the older Bantu languages, or that it was borrowed from the later dialects. In Nano, Angola, Kongo, Mpongwe, it does not seem to exist; in Dualla most of the words beginning with *bu* are "concrete" objects, in which *bu* really belongs to the *stem* of the noun (*e.g.* in *boso* = face, and *bolo* = ship), and in such words as *bosangi* = cleanliness, and *bubi* = sin, the prefix may have been borrowed with the word from other Bantu tribes.

In Luganda the *bu* class of nouns comprises a large amount of "concrete," as well as "abstract" nouns, and this is easily accounted for by the fact that *Luganda*, though originally the headquarters of the *first* Bantu invaders, became also the headquarters of the *second* Bantu invaders, and was thus liable to adopt several Sumerian-Babylonian words in its later vocabulary.

Hence I am inclined to think that the prefix *bu* is directly connected with the Babylonian *banu* = to form, and more particularly with the noun derived herefrom, *bunu*, which means "outward appearance, form," and especially "face." In fact, in the latter meaning the root is found in a very generally used Bantu word, which in Zulu is *ubuso*, a word which is, through false analogy, supposed to have the prefix *bu*, but which is really *u-buso*.* The prefix would thus express the "form" or "outward appearance" of matters, and would lend itself perfectly to describe what we call "abstract nouns" by giving "a form" in language to things which have no form in nature. So *ubu-ntu* = mankind would be "the general form of man"; *ubu-de* = length, would be the "form of being long."

As in all other prefixes, a considerable amount of misunderstanding has arisen about this prefix, due to "false analogy." Thus *utywoala* = beer, is given in the new Kafir Grammar of the Rev. J. McLaren as a palatised form of an original *ubu-ala*, while Bleek in his "Comparative Grammar," p. 154, seems to consider that the *u* stands for an original *ubu*, as this prefix appears in the Zulu form *ubu-tywala*. It is probable that the newer form of the word is *ubutywala*, as would seem from Secwana *bo-yaloa*. The root of the word is *tywala*, which is the regular Zulu form of the old Baluchi *juara* = kafircorn (*Sorghum vulgare*), under which name this plant is known over the greater part of India. *Ubutywala* (for original *ubu-juara*) would thus correctly represent "that which is made from *juara*," and this is strong evidence in favour of my explanation of the original meaning of the prefix *bu*. On the

---

*It need scarcely be said that this *buso* = face is not *derived* from Babylonian, but from the ancient Ugro-Altaic language, as is proved by Sakai *balo* = face, Sirjenish *ban* = face, front; Votian *ban* = face.

other hand, *u-tyani*=pasture in Kafir is not, as McLaren thinks, a form of *ubu-ani*, but stands for an original *u-sani* (*ty*=*s*), from the Sumerian *se-in-nu* = forage, grain, straw, and has only the ordinary article *u* as a prefix.

The more I study Bantu, the more do I become convinced that our ideas of the Bantu prefixes require thorough and careful revision, and that from a philological point of view we cannot implicitly trust to the actual conditions under which the Bantu themselves apply these prefixes. It is clear that the Bantu have absolutely forgotten the origin and effect of these prefixes, and, being led astray by false analogy and popular etymology, have made " a fair mess " of their own language, even more so than the Englishman does, when he considers such words as *alms* and *riches* as true plurals.

I may, *e.g.*, quote here a very pretty example with reference to the supposed prefix *si* or *se* denoting languages in Bantu. *Mosuto* is one man of the Sutu tribe ; *Ba-suto* is the plural, and *Se-suto* is the language of that tribe. *Mo-shuana* is one man of the *Shuana* (now often written *cwana*) tribe ; *Be-shuana* is the plural ; *Se-shuana* is the language. So Grout has *I-si-zulu* for the Zulu language. Bantu grammarians represent, therefore, that for the *single* individual we use the first prefix, for the plural the second, and for the language the seventh prefix. This statement shows, with all due respect, how crude our notions of Bantu philology are as yet.

The *se* or *si* used in front of the tribal name, to denote the *language*, is no prefix at all, but is the old Ugro-Altaic word for *language*, and is found in nearly all existing languages of that group.

In Semang we have *chu*=to talk, and *sua*=voice. Sirjenish has *si*=word, voice, and *sua*=to speak. Jakutish has *sej*=voice ; Manchu has *se-mbi* (where *mbi* is simply a verbal *affix*)=to speak ; Turkish has *suz*=word ; Japanese has *ji*=word, and *se-tsu*=talk (*noun*). Several non-Aryan languages of India have *che-wa*=to speak, as well as *je*, *su-ang* and *su-u* in the same meaning, which are all from the same root. Finnish has *sa-na*=word ; Magyar has *so*=sound, voice, speech ; Sumerian has *zag*=speech, and evidently a *si* form, from which the Assyrian *si-ku*=speech and *si-ku-ru*=to speak, were derived.

From the above it is clear that the *si* or *se* in Bantu is evidently the word for "language." In certain Bantu groups (Suaheli, Kamba, etc.) we have the prefix *ki*, and this prefix is strong proof for our theory. For while *si* or *se* is derived from the Semang *chu* and *sua*, *ki* is derived from the Sakai *kui*=language, speech, which root is also found in Japanese *kuchi*=to demand, and *kotoba*=language, in Mandchu *kumun*=music ;

in Finnish *pu-hua* = to speak, and probably in Talien (one of the Indian languages) *han-kai* = to speak, and in Sumerian *ku*.*

IX. The ninth prefix *in* is in reality no prefix at all, but simply the article in its *i* form with nasalisation or better *nunation*, and that same nunation also appears in the plural or tenth prefix *izin*, which is the eighth prefix.

III. and IV. Lastly, there remain the third and fourth pre-fixes to be discussed, viz., *mu* and *mi*.

It seems to me that the words which compose the third class are a very *heterogeneous* mixture. In many of the words of this class, the *mu* is exactly the same as the *mu* of the first class. *Umu-zi* = village, is nothing else but the article *u*, the prefix *mu* = man, and the root *zi* = dwelling, found in Sakai *si-ar* and *si-au* = hut, house, dwelling, in some Indian dialects and in several Ugro-Altaic languages, the real original root being *sa* = spot, place. *Umuti* = tree (after which word this class has been erroneously termed the " tree " class by some writers) has no prefix *mu* at all. The *mu* here forms part of the root of the word, and represents the old Turanian *mi* (*mai, mo, mu*) = fire, found in a very large number of non-Aryan languages. Trees were considered as " things to burn," and the two ideas of " fire " and " tree " are intimately connected. In some Indian languages (*e.g.* Southal, Singpo Kol, Bhumi and others) *sengel* = fire; while in Dhimal, Chepang, Cchi-tangya, and many others, *sing* or *sang* is " tree," and in Zulu we find the latter root in *isinga* = a forest. In the same way Somali *mi* = forest is connected with *mi* = fire, and Mang'anja *moti* = fire, with *umuti* = tree. In Burjetian we find *modo* = tree, and in Manchu the same word is *moo*, while Annamese, one of the purest Mon-Khmer languages, has *muk* = tree. From the latter word it is perfectly clear that the *mu* in *umuti* forms a part of the root of the word. In words like *umoya* there is no prefix *mu*, and the *mo* belongs to the stem of the root-word (see above), and the *u* is the real prefix, or rather article. In Kafir *um-lambo* (= umulambo) = river, we have the prefix *mu* = man and the root *lam* = way, road, and a river was thus defined as " a road for man," a definition actually found not only in Semang, but in several Indian languages, where the ideas " road " and " river " are apparently confused, or very intimately connected.

---

*This *ku* appears, *inter alia*, in *eme-ku*. This *eme-ku* with its counterpart *eme-sal*, which together form the *two* languages of old Sumir has puzzled all Assyriologists so far, and Prince, in his *Sumerian Lexicon*, pp. 13-15, has given explanations which are very far-fetched. If Sumerian students had gone somewhat further afield, they would have come to the very evident conclusion that *eme-ku* is the " spoken, ordinary language," the language of daily life, while *eme-sal* is the " higher, written language, used in inscriptions and gov-ernment decrees. *Sal* is connected with Semang *sur-at* = to write, Ao-Naga *zilu* = to write, Angami-Naga *thu* (th = z) = to write ; Turkish *zabtet* ; Japanese *suri* = to print (" to rub ink on a stone ") ; Manchu *selgiyembi* = to publish ; Japanese *sho suru* = to write ; Buretian *zuranam* = to make strokes.

In *um* as a prefix for rivers in both Kafir and Zulu (*Um-* *zimvubu*, *Umvolosi*, etc.) the *um* has absolutely nothing to do with the prefix *mu*, but this *um* is the shortened and metathised word for ancient Semang *munun* = a " ford," still found in Burjetian *umbanap* = to wade, and, perhaps, with Sumerian *mu-un*, which Prince, *op. cit.*, p. 244, explains as " what binds together the land."

I believe that, fairly well the half of class 3 consists of " false analogies," and to do justice to the subject one should carefully examine every word in this class, which cannot be done here.

The plural form, or fourth prefix *imi*, I consider to be a mere changed form of *ama*, in accordance with the " concord of vowels ' so common in old Bantu.

In conclusion, I beg to reiterate my opinion that the prefixes in Bantu require very careful examination, and that the rules and principles now generally accepted should be carefully tested. Careless work on the part of authors has certainly complicated matters to a large extent, and independent research is absolutely required.* The old theories, I am afraid, will have to be gradually discarded, and we must look at Bantu, its prefixes, its inflections, and its very highly developed forms in a different light than we have done thus far.

SECTION X.

Having given in the former paragraph what I consider the natural and correct view of the Bantu prefixes, and the only one in harmony with the historical development of this language group, the next question to be solved is the *Concord* in Bantu.

Like the prefixes, the Concord has been thus far considered a linguistic phenomenon exclusively Bantu, except in so far as Bleek has attempted to show that this Concord existed, to a certain extent, in the Hottentot language. I am not prepared to discuss this latter matter, which forms a subject in itself. But there can be no doubt, that the Concord, as found in Bantu, is certainly specifically a matter which has developed in that language group itself, though the germs may be found in earlier languages.

As an appendix to the first volume of their oft-quoted work on the Pagan Races of the Malay Peninsula, Messrs. Skeat and Blagden have given us a number of Besisi and Blanda songs. I

------

*As a specimen of the careless way in which Bantu is handled I may quote a book, called " Elements of Luganda Grammar," written by a missionary in Uganda. There I find on page 48, *ekitabo* = book, given as a noun of the *ki* class (*sic*) ! Naturally *ekitabo* is the Bantuised form of Arabian *kitab* = book, and the prefix is *e* and not *eki*. Such things are bound to make Bantu " confusion worse confounded."

have carefully gone into these, but I must confess that, though I have found a good deal of " repetition of words," I have found nothing like Concord, or even Alliteration, in them. Unfortunately, I have not been able to obtain any songs of the non-Aryan tribes of India, and I am thus unable to say whether the germs of Concord are found there.

Before, however, entering into this question historically, we might first ask another question, viz., " What is Concord ? "

My answer to this is : " *Concord* is *Alliteration* systemised in such a manner that the alliteration is dependent upon the *consonants*, or any *particular consonant*, of the word, which expresses the leading idea in the sentence. Usually that leading idea is contained in the *subject* of the sentence. Under special circumstances the Concord can depend upon the *vowel* of the leading word in the sentence."

I have just now called Concord a *linguistic phenomenon*, but in reality this is a misnomer, for Concord has really nothing to do with speech. *Speech* is connected primarily with the tongue, the teeth, the throat, the palate, and the various *oral* organs ; *Alliteration* and *Concord* are solely connected with the *ear*, and hence it should be classed as a *musical phenomenon*. Alliteration originated in Poetry, when Poetry was pure and simple song. There is no doubt that originally such songs were connected with religious rites.

The musical faculty in the Bantu is splendidly developed and, as a rule, they have a remarkably good ear. That is, to a certain extent, one of the reasons why the Bantu have developed the Concord to such a remarkable degree.

In his " Kilima-Njara Expedition " (London, 1886), p. 460, Sir H. H. Johnston, then, as it were, at the commencement of his brilliant career, has attempted to show that there exists a kind of Concord in Galla, and even in Arabic. But it is a question open to doubt whether this Concord is the same as that of the Bantu.

Placed as I am, I have not been able to obtain access to any important ancient Ugro-Altaic poetry, or even to Sumerian poetry. But the " Great Epic of Gilgamesh," with its magnificent Legend of the Deluge, was undoubtedly originally a Sumerian production, of which we only possess to-day the Babylonian adaptation. But even in that adaptation we find clear traces of *alliteration*, showing that the Semitic translator tried to introduce into Semitic a non-Semitic principle. In the following passages, taken from the " Legend of the Deluge," as found in Rosenberg's " Assyrische Sprachlehre (Hartleben)," Vienna, p. 60 and ff., some examples of this attempt are given :
Line 13.

Alu su-u labürma ilaani kirbusu.

(r and l being always interchangeable, would naturally fall under the same principle of alliteration.)

Line 27.

Su*l*ima zee*er* naapsaati ka*l*ama ana *l*ibbi e*l*üppi.

Line 83.

Miimma isuu esiensi huraasu.

Line 85.

Uste*l*i ana *l*iibbi e*l*üppi ka*l*a kümtüa u sa*l*atüa.

Line 147.

U*s*esima *s*uummatu umaassür.

Line 163.

T*l*aani u*ll*anuumma Bee*l*it i*l*aani ina kasadisu.

I have just picked out a few of the most prominent examples, but many more might be quoted from the same poem, and it seems evident that the Assyrian poet attempted to imitate the alliteration of the Sumerian original, as far as the Semitic language allowed him to do so.

Not having been able to obtain access to any Sumerian poetry (a fact which has undoubtedly handicapped me considerably) I had recourse to what is perhaps the nearest to it, namely, the magnificent poetry of the Finns, as found in the " Kalevala." The whole of tltis great epic I could not obtain, but luckily I found many extracts from it in A. Castren's " Vorlesungen uber die Finnische Mythologie " (translated by A. Schiefner), a copy of which is possessed by the S.A. Library in Cape Town. What I saw there was more than sufficient for my purpose. For there I found not only pure *Alliteration*, but actually the " first dawnings " of the Bantu Concord. I shall only quote a few verses, in the original, without giving Schiefner's German translations, because the only object is to show how perfectly this alliteration exists in Finnish poetry :

    I. Anna ucko uuhiansi
       Anna oinahat omansi
       Ukko kullainen kuningas
       Tuuvos ilman tuusimata
       Varomata vaaputtele.

    II. Pikkuisessa pirttisessä
       Kamarissa kaituisessa
       Kiven kirjavan kylessa
       Paaen paksun kainalossa.

    III. Vaski oli hattu hartioilla
       Vaski saappahat jalassa
       Vaski kirjat kintahissa
       Vaski-vyövyt vyölle vyötty
       Vaski kirves vyön takana.

IV. Kaistat kalaisen karjan
Tämän nuotan nostimille,
Sata-lauan laskimille
Kalaisista kaartehista,
Lohisista loukeroista,
Suurilta selän navoilta,
Synkiltä syväntehiltä,
Täivän paistamattomilta,
Hiekan hieromattomilta.

V. Sorea on suonten vaimo
Suanetar sorea vaimo
Soma suonten kehreäjä
Sorealla kehrinpuulla
Vaskisella vätrtinällä
Rautaisella rattahalla
Tule tänne tarvitaissa
Käy tänne kutsuttaessa
Suoni sykkyrä sylissä
Kalvo kääri kainalossa
Suonia sitelemähän
Päitä suonten solmimahan
Haavoissa halennehissa
Rei'issä revennehissä !

Surely we have here alliteration with a vengeance ! But have
we here the Bantu concord ?

In Bantu the Concord consists of *alliteration* dependent upon
the *prefix* of the *subject* of the sentence, or better, of the word
expressing the leading idea of the sentence.   But leaving the
consideration of the prefix question aside for the moment, the
Bantu concord is dependent practically upon the *first letter* of
the leading word (excluding the article).   Thus in the Zulu
sentence given by Bleek, page 97 :

"A*b*antu *b*etu a*b*achle *b*aya-*b*onakala si*b*atanda,"

the " concord " is dependent upon the *first* letter of the word
bantu, which is the subject of the principal sentence, and con-
veys the leading idea of the sentence.

In the Finnish examples given above we find in most cases
an *alliteration* of the initial consonant (and even in the first two
lines of Example I. of the vowels).   In nearly all cases, the
alliteration is dependent upon the leading word in the sentence.
So in Example II. all the first words are the nouns with which
the verb " to sit," in the first two lines (root form *istua*) agrees,
while in the two last lines the adjectives " gaudy " and " thick "
also agree with the nouns.   This is very clear in Example III.,
where the leading word is *vaski* = copper, and in the first line
the concord is with the letter *i* of the word, in the second with

the s, in the third with the k, in the fourth with the initial v, and in the last with both v and k, the initial letters of the two syllables of Vas-ki, a very pretty piece of poetical alliteration.

In the IV. Example the concord agrees all through with the leading idea in each line, though the word expressing it does not in every case stand at the beginning of the line, but sometimes, like *karjan* ("flock" or here "shoal of fishes"), stands at the back.

We have thus here in Finnish something which comes very near the Concord in Bantu, though as appears from the examples given, in Finnish that principle is not always carried through with the unswerving consistency found in Zulu, Kafir, and most of the other Bantu languages.

It is, therefore, very probable that the "Concord" as it exists to-day in Bantu was developed and brought to its present musical perfection within the Bantu itself, after the tribes had settled in Africa. The facts that the Bantu had lost the art of writing, that all great events were commemorated in songs, and that in honour of their chief they sung "his great names," and his prowess, as the Zulu still did in the times of Tjaka and Dingaan, and several Bantu tribes in Central Africa are now accustomed to do, would greatly tend to develop the Concord, which, as we have seen above, existed already in Ugro-Altaic. That very fact of not possessing the art of writing, together with the inborn love for musical sounds which the Bantu have, was undoubtedly the cause that the *Concord* was applied to the ordinary prose language of daily life, and thus gradually became a great *linguistic* factor.

Under the present circumstances, and within the necessarily narrow limits of this sketch of the Bantu origin, I cannot enter more deeply upon this question of Concord, a matter which really requires a volume in itself. For at present, the Concord constitutes, as it were, the grammatical centre around which the whole of the Bantu turns, and a consideration thereof would lead us too far away out of my course. What has been said above tends, however, to strengthen the bond which, I maintain, exists between Bantu and Ugro-Altaic.

In conclusion, a few words regarding this relation may not be out of place.

To many it might seem absurd to connect the semi-, or sometimes wholly, savage Bantu with the highly-developed Finn, or the energetic and pushing Japanese, but it should be remembered that in the Finn, the Sirjenian, the Votian and all the other members of the Finnish group, we have probably a strong Aryan element ; that in the Manchu and the Japanese we have a specifically-developed *Jakun* element, which we generally denominate *Mongolian*, but the history of which is still shrouded in mystery ; that, again, in the blood of the "unspeakable Turk," and his relations, we have a strong Semitic strain, and perhaps some Aryan drops.

The Bantu miss that foreign element. In them there is probably no other blood than that of the *Sakai* and the *Semang*, of the old Nagas or Lu, who ages ago populated India, but who, after the Aryan conquest, seem to have made their headquarters the present Beluchistan, and perhaps part of Afghanistan. But before these Nagas could enter upon a new development, the Bantu, who in any case seem to have belonged to a low Naga division, or may have even been outcasts, left the country and started life anew in Africa. While in the original home their brethren rose, step by step, in civilisation, and sent off branch after branch northwards to populate nearly the whole of Asia north of the Himalaya, the Bantu in Africa entered upon a career which could only have a most baneful effect upon their development. In a strange country, where Nature was fitful, where one year the earth produced plenty, and the next even a drop of water might be a boon ; having to struggle for an existence not only with Nature, but also with human enemies, who surrounded them on all sides ; split up in course of time in various divisions, whose sole object in life was to prey upon each other, as to-day is still done by his relatives in Beluchistan ; possessors of fertile lands to-day, and wanderers in the desert to-morrow—is it a wonder that, under such circumstances, the Bantu sank lower and lower in the scale of civilisation ? Low they did sink ; in some cases they even reached cannibalism. Yet they never sank to the depths that the Hottentot sank in the Bushman type ; they never became isolated nomads, but always kept their *tribal system* in full force. And it is this tribal system, with all its remarkable institutions, social as well as political, which saved the Bantu from utter deterioration. Immense charms as this aspect of the Bantu has, I cannot discuss it here, but must leave that for a more fitting opportunity.

In the above essay, an attempt has been made, clumsily perhaps, to find a key which will open to us the secret of Bantu philology not only, but the hidden mysteries of Bantu character and Bantu institutions. As such this essay is, what I have called it, a *preliminary* work. The *key* I have tried to find must be tested ; we must see whether it will fit upon the locks of the great safe which holds what we wish to see and observe for ourselves.

The few years of the rest of my life I intend to devote to this task or, at all events, to some small part of it. Whether I shall be enabled to carry out this intention depends, to a large extent, upon others. For such work one must have not only leisure, but one must be enabled to devote his whole energy to it, and hence it is necessary that some provision should be made for the sordid cares of mere animal existence.

But the work cannot be done by *one* man, even if he had half a century at his disposal. We want workers, earnest, capable, and enthusiastic workers in this field ; we want a number of them.

If this essay should be fortunate enough to induce some of our smart young South Africans, who now grace the roll of our University calendars, to join the rank of workers in the study of Bantu philology, Bantu institutions, and the kindred subjects, the writer will consider himself amply rewarded for the innumerable hours of close and hard study he has devoted to this little work. Then only will he feel the truth of the motto of a noble English family—

PER ASPERA AD ASTRA.

[G.17 — 1907.]

CPSIA information can be obtained
at www.ICGtesting.com
Printed in the USA
BVHW09*1549220818
525303BV00006B/86/P

9 780266 910930